# THE
# ACCIDENTAL
# SHAMAN

---

"The author's honest narration of his long exploration of South American shamanism is a delight to read. Valuable insights from an author who walks his talk."

NICHOLAS BREEZE WOOD,
EDITOR OF *SACRED HOOP* MAGAZINE

"The author tells insightful shamanic stories based on personal experience while recognizing the wisdom of indigenous cultures. His book also contains precious wisdom regarding safety in contemporary shamanic practices."

JEREMY NARBY, ANTHROPOLOGIST AND AUTHOR OF
*THE COSMIC SERPENT: DNA AND THE ORIGINS OF KNOWLEDGE*
AND *INTELLIGENCE IN NATURE*

"Although the author refers to himself as "the Accidental Shaman" it becomes very clear from his shocking elevator crash to his stunning encounters with the indigenous people and their medicines that Howard G. Charing was chosen by powerful spiritual forces beyond his own ego control to walk the shamanic path of death and rebirth. His miraculous transformational journey has manifested in his being able to share his gifts with others also in need of deep healing."

LINDA STAR WOLF, PH.D. IN SHAMANIC PSYCHOSPIRITUAL STUDIES AND AUTHOR OF *SOUL WHISPERING: THE ART OF AWAKENING SHAMANIC CONSCIOUSNESS*

"A must-read for anyone wanting to explore unseen worlds! Powerful shamanic wisdom that will guide you on how to consciously connect more fully with energy fields and the spirit world."

ROBBIE HOLZ, COAUTHOR OF *SECRETS OF ABORIGINAL HEALING* AND *ABORIGINAL SECRETS OF AWAKENING*

# THE
# ACCIDENTAL
# SHAMAN

## Journeys with Plant Teachers and Other Spirit Allies

## Howard G. Charing

Destiny Books
Rochester, Vermont • Toronto, Canada

Destiny Books
One Park Street
Rochester, Vermont 05767
www.DestinyBooks.com

Text stock is SFI certified

Destiny Books is a division of Inner Traditions International

Copyright © 2017 by Howard G. Charing

**Library of Congress Cataloging-in-Publication Data**

Names: Charing, Howard G., author.
Title: The accidental shaman : journeys with plant teachers and other spirit allies / Howard G. Charing.
Description: Rochester, Vermont : Destiny Books, 2017. | Includes index.
Identifiers: LCCN 2016034918 (print) | LCCN 2017001800 (e-book) | ISBN 9781620556092 (pbk.) | ISBN 9781620556108 (e-book)
Subjects: LCSH: Shamanism. | Spiritual healing—Shamanism. | Plants—Religious aspects—Shamanism.
Classification: LCC BF1611 .C465 2017 (print) | LCC BF1611 (e-book) | DDC 201/.44—dc23
LC record available at https://lccn.loc.gov/2016034918

Printed and bound in the United States by Lake Book Manufacturing, Inc. The text stock is SFI certified. The Sustainable Forestry Initiative® program promotes sustainable forest management.

10 9 8 7 6 5 4 3 2 1

Text design and layout by Priscilla Baker
This book was typeset in Garamond Premier Pro with Plat, Gill Sans, Legacy Sans, and Avant Garde used as display typefaces

To send correspondence to the author of this book, mail a first-class letter to the author c/o Inner Traditions • Bear & Company, One Park Street, Rochester, VT 05767, and we will forward the communication, or contact the author directly at **www.shamanism.co.uk**.

# CONTENTS

✳

# FOREWORD

*Never allow your reality to be undermined.*

HOWARD G. CHARING

I honestly can't remember when I first met Howard. He comes and goes a lot, as many shamans do. I remember he once stayed in my house for a week or so as he was traveling around the United States. My house is set on a busy urban street just a few blocks from a popular beach and zoo. We would sit on my front stoop while he smoked his morning cigar, and together we would watch the summer parade of people on the street. I remember how delighted he was to find an old-fashioned barbershop just up the block.

We talked together for hours, about *everything*. I discovered a man who was deeply knowledgeable about shamanism around the world, particularly the shamanism of the Upper Amazon, a culture in which he had immersed himself for many years. He had long experience working with shamans in the region; he had published dozens of interviews with them. We found that we knew many of the same people; we shared our knowledge of jungle lore, traded stories of shamans both impeccable and perfidious, and spoke especially of his love and admiration for the shaman and visionary artist Pablo Amaringo.

I became aware of something that you will find to be true throughout this book: Howard is an enthralling storyteller. If you love stories—that is, if you are a human being—you are in for a treat.

It is easy to believe that Howard has been just about everywhere. He has performed psychic surgery in the Philippines, worked with some of the most respected shamans in the Amazon, produced intricate and colorful ayahuasca-inspired paintings, and was initiated into the lineage of the maestros of the Rio Napo in the Upper Amazon. He is now in Romania, living in Transylvania (not far from Castle Dracula), studying Romanian shamanism. I am not surprised.

It is important, I think, to underscore Howard's unstinting devotion to what he calls the "Great Domain." His first book was on Amazonian plant spirit medicine, for which Pablo Amaringo wrote the foreword. This was the start of an epic and productive collaboration. When Amaringo died in 2009, he left behind a mass of uncataloged paintings and hastily jotted notes. Howard, along with Peter Cloudsley, had been working with Amaringo for months to get his collection in order, annotate his more recent work, create a digital archive of his art, and protect his paintings from deterioration in their humid tropical environment. The meticulously cataloged and annotated collection became the basis for the remarkable and beautiful posthumous book *The Ayahuasca Visions of Pablo Amaringo*.

The book you now hold in your hands is another treasure. It is a storehouse of Howard's knowledge, experience, and teaching. But it is more.

Psychologist James Hillman distinguishes between two basic orientations to the world, which he calls *spirit* and *soul*. Spirit, he says, is detached, objective, intense, absolute, abstract, pure, metaphysical, clear, unitary, eternal, and heavenly. Soul, on the other hand, is mortal, earthly, low, troubled, sorrowful, vulnerable, melancholy, weak, dependent, and profound. *Spirit* means fire and height, the center of things; *soul* means water and depth, peripheries, borderlands. Spirit seeks to transcend earth and body, dirt and disease, entanglements and complications, perplexity and despair, "seeks to escape or transcend the pleasures and demands of ordinary earthly life."[1] But soul, as Thomas Moore puts it in his anthology of Hillman's writings, "is always in the thick of things: in the repressed, in the shadow, in the messes of life, in illness, and in the pain and confusion of love."[2]

It is soul, not spirit, that is the true landscape of shamanism—the landscape of suffering, passion, and mess. Shamans deal with sickness, envy, malice, conflict, bad luck, hatred, despair, and death. Indeed, the purpose of the shaman is to dwell in the valley of the soul—to heal what has been broken in the body and the community. Shamans live with betrayal, loss, confusion, need, and failure—including their own.

In this book we have a remarkably forthright and detailed chronicle of such a shaman *at work*. Howard is first and foremost a healer and visionary, clearly situated in the valley of the soul, and he shares with us his visions, his practices, and his remarkable experiences. At the same time, we can watch him *thinking through* his healing practices and experiences, placing them within a wider—indeed, a global—context. He is a man at the intersection of many forms of shamanism, drawn together by his personal healing mission.

This is really three books in one. The first is Howard's fascinating story, from the shattering accident that opened up his healing visions, to his meetings with teachers and shamans, to his own healing experiences and practices. The second is his exploration of what these experiences *mean*, his exploration of how these experiences and healings fit into a variety of current understandings of shamanism worldwide. And, third, the book is in itself a shamanic tutor, incorporating a number of exploratory exercises deriving from Howard's many years of leading workshops around the world.

The book is the story of a modern Westerner discovering a healing gift, learning to use it, and striving to understand it. It is valuable for us all.

STEPHAN V. BEYER, PH.D.

Stephan V. Beyer—researcher in ethnomedicine, shamanism, peacemaking, and the spirituality of nonviolence—studied wilderness survival among the indigenous peoples of North and South America, and sacred plant medicine with traditional herbalists in North America and *curanderos* (healers) in the Upper Amazon. With a law degree and doctorates in both Buddhist studies and psychology, Steve has been a university professor, a trial lawyer, a wilderness guide, and a peacemaker and community builder. He lived for a year and a half in a Tibetan monastery in the Himalayas and has undertaken and helped to lead numerous four-day and four-night solo vision fasts in the desert wildernesses of New Mexico. The Institute for the Preservation of Medical Traditions at the Smithsonian Institution has written, "Stephan Beyer . . . has an unparalleled knowledge of sacred plants." He is the author of several books, including *Singing to the Plants: A Guide to Mestizo Shamanism in the Upper Amazon* and, most recently, *Talking Stick: Peacemaking as a Spiritual Path*.

✳

# ACKNOWLEDGMENTS

I would like to offer my thanks and heart-filled appreciation to those who have helped, challenged, and inspired me on this ongoing journey, in particular, Leo Rutherford, Pablo Amaringo, Peter Cloudsley, John-Richard Turner, and Steve Beyer. In addition, I also thank the indigenous shamans and healers with whom I have worked over the years and who have been generous in sharing their knowledge and medicine teachings.

$*$

# INTRODUCTION

*To boldly go where no one has gone before...*

*STAR TREK*

mong the first questions a prospective reader of a nonfiction book asks, whether implicitly or explicitly, are: Will this book be interesting and useful to me? Will I learn something? Can it inspire me in some way? Of course, these are difficult questions to answer, as they are matters of individual subjectivity. However, one thing I have learned over the years is that people can be reached by, can identify with, and can even have their soul touched by a personal story or narrative. This is what this book offers: a woven tapestry, a blending of my personal journeys and adventures that began more than thirty years ago with a near-death experience and years of physical disability caused by an elevator crash. The main purpose of this nonfiction narrative is to provide background texture and context for insights, perspectives, and practices to inspire, to stimulate, and ultimately to encourage readers in their unique life adventures. From this viewpoint, my own experiences are, I hope, empowering gifts to the readers. This book is also somewhat of a hybrid; it weaves together a personal travelogue and my various observations and post hoc insights concerning these experiences, and includes exercises and practices so that readers can explore shamanism themselves.

As it happens, this was far from my original intention when I started to write this book. I have gathered a lot of material over the years, and my idea was to go in the direction of a third-party, somewhat dispassionate standpoint. The original working title for this book was "The Shaman's This and That." In many respects that was the approach I had taken with my previous books, *Plant Spirit Shamanism* and *The Ayahuasca Visions of Pablo Amaringo*.

So I began writing from that neutral perspective, and then a few months down the road, I was taking a shower, when suddenly the "voice" (which you will read more about in the book) spoke out loud and said, "Change the book title to *The Accidental Shaman*." I was quite stunned. It was a great title with a double meaning (after all, I just love word play and puns). After the shower I started to seriously consider this new title and its implications. Titles are important because they set both the tone and the purpose of a book. I realized that the entire emphasis of the book would need to change, with a considerable amount of rewriting required to bring the material into accord with the title. It was unnerving without a doubt because I came to realize that my mistakes, my screw ups, and a host of messy situations that I had become involved in along my journey would have to be included. I know that a biographical narrative has to be presented without any gloss or cosmetic ornamentation if you are expressing a true story (warts and all, so to speak) to engage honestly with the readers. So I gritted my teeth and got on with it, with some nail biting along the way. Here are the results of that endeavor.

Obviously, I am aware of the exquisite irony of reading books about spiritual transformation, enlightenment, personal development, and discovering one's purpose in life. This is part of Western culture, a way to seek out wisdom, knowledge, and an understanding that there is indeed far more to reality than we have been taught or shown. I see this as our inner (or soul's) desire to fully engage and immerse our being in the duality of our physical, material world and the ineffable, incorporeal realms of higher order, or universal, consciousness. Therein lies the rub (to misquote Shakespeare): the quest for true wisdom and personal enlightenment can never come from words in a book or from other people's descriptions of their experiences. I can unequivocally state that true wisdom can only be consummated through navigating our personal journeys, gathering our individual experiences, and learning (in my case, by trial and error) how to live a life of purpose, fulfillment, and empowerment, walking in beauty and grace in this precious world.

My great teacher and maestro, the Amazonian shaman and visionary artist Pablo Amaringo, expressed this in his distinctive way when he discussed with me the difference between *knowledge* and *wisdom*. He said, "Love is not *gnosis* (knowledge), but *epignosis* (above knowledge). You can read all the literature about ayahuasca, understand its chemical composition and so on—this is gnosis; but only when you drink it [ayahuasca] is there the possibility of realization of this knowledge, or epignosis."[1]

From a broader philosophical perspective, the transformative change is already happening. Humanity is at a threshold; a future beckons of human-created catastrophic ecological changes, vehement religious fundamentalism, and unparalleled technological advancement. These present massive social, economic, and spiritual challenges that either we or our children will have to face. In this turbulent vortex of entropy, we can be sure that much that we hold dear will collapse; yet out of this turmoil a new world can emerge, much like the archetypal myth of regeneration, the phoenix rising from the ashes.

Humanity is eminently adaptable and resourceful, and I look to the future with a heart-filled sense of optimism. A clear and tangible generational shift is taking place; people in their teens and twenties hold a new vibrant frequency. This is the frequency of interconnectivity, transparency, and global awareness, incorporating humanity with the natural world. This creative evolution is accelerating, and more people than ever are growing the seed of evolving consciousness within. Everything is in place, the cast is assembled, and the stage is set for what will be a breathtaking, magnificent, and electrifying journey to a new paradigm. I may not be here to witness the outcome, and so I offer my blessings to you in this time of growth and transformation.

A book is like a living thing; it has a conception, gestation, birth, and development. Then it is ready to go out into the world, to inform, to inspire, to challenge, or simply to offer a different perspective. If this book achieves any of these objectives then that will be truly gratifying.

# 1

# THE ACCIDENT

*I don't believe in accidents. There are only encounters in history. There are no accidents.*

PABLO PICASSO

It was a beautiful spring day in 1983. I was on vacation with Shelley, my wife, in Verona at the Piazza Brà, drinking an espresso and admiring the ancient Roman amphitheater. This was where we met Aaron. I was drinking my coffee when I suddenly heard a loud commotion. Looking behind me I could see people crowding around a man who was clearly having a seizure. It was as if an invisible pile driver was pounding his body into the ground; his body was moving downward with massive staccato jolts. His convulsing body was surrounded by a mass of people, who were making a lot of noise in their distress. Police officers joined the bystanders but seemed unable to offer any assistance.

As I sat watching this drama, I heard a man at an adjacent table express his disapproval of the scene. I turned around and gestured with my arms up and hands open to indicate a kind of helplessness with the situation. He looked at me with a probing but not unfriendly intensity, and then he very politely asked in perfect English if he could join us at our table. We said, "Yes, please do." We shook hands and introduced ourselves as he sat with us. He had a dignified appearance, this man in his mid- to late forties with grayish white hair and suntanned olive skin. This was Aaron, a man who would change my life.

I asked him why he was angry. He turned and pointed to the scene. The collapsed man by now had a swarm of people around him; the police were finally starting to get a grip on the situation and were pushing people back to enable the man to have some breathing and recovery space. Aaron said, "I am angry because there is a doctor at one of the tables, but he does not want to get involved." I asked, "How do you know this?" He then drew his chair closer and studied me, and I felt as if I was being scrutinized. He started to speak, and for the next hour I sat transfixed, as if I was in the grip of a magical enchantment. He told me about my life, my dreams, my hopes, and my dark and painful experiences. It was if I had become an open book, and my inner secrets were being revealed page by page.

The background noise faded away, and unexpressed emotions began welling up from within me. Tears rolled down my face. He paused for a moment and signaled to a waiter for more coffee while I attempted to regroup and assimilate what had happened. We sat for a few moments in silence and drank our coffee as I tried to recover my former confident and relaxed composure.

He then said, "Our meeting was not simply chance. I am one of the most well-known psychic healers in Italy." He expanded his arms. "People come from all over Europe to consult me for healing." He pointed at me and said, "You!" It looked as if he was searching for a word, and then he continued, "are a very good person and you will be doing the same work that I am doing."

The coffee had enabled me to get my composure back, and I quickly dismissed this. He looked at me with a stern expression and responded, "This is a serious matter, and I do not make jokes about this!" As I was absorbing this, he said, "I will now give you a blessing." He placed his hand on the top of my head and spoke softly in Italian. As he was making his blessing, my body felt like a cauldron, with liquid fire burning within and moving upward. Waves of energy pulsated through me, and intense heat flowed from my spine, up through my head and down to my shoulders, along my arms, and into my hands, which now felt as if they were red hot.

Shelley was watching this exchange with total incredulity and said, "This is nonsense!" Aaron looked at her and gently replied, "You will be presenting Howard with a baby." Shelley burst into tears and didn't say a further word. She was no longer skeptical because we had been trying for a while to start a family.

Later he invited us to dinner with his family and gave us a wonderful tour of Verona, complete with a visit to the balcony of the Casa di Giulietta that recreates the romance of Romeo and Juliet. Before we took our leave of each other, he presented us with gifts, including bottles of wine. His final words were "Our work with you is done," and we fondly said our farewells.

A week later I was back in London at my place of business. I entered the elevator and pushed the button to go up. Suddenly my stomach flew into my mouth, and an enormous force began crushing me. The lift was out of control and plummeting at great speed. I knew without a shred of doubt that then and there I was going to die. As soon as I realized this, I was gone, out and away, soaring from my body, which became infinitesimal as it receded in the distance. Then I was *somewhere,* disembodied in an indescribable "other" place. This place pulsed with colored waves of light, and I knew that I had to make a decision, to either live or die, and I decided not to die. As soon as I made the decision to live, I was back in my physical body.

Time stopped for me, and the world stood still. I found myself calmly looking down at my body, and it felt as if I had all the time in the world. I thought I must be able to do something! I tried jumping up (something that I had seen in the Road Runner cartoons), but I couldn't move upward; the law of gravity did not permit that. And then suddenly I knew with total certainty precisely what to do. I got into a crouch position, took out my handkerchief, and shoved it into my mouth. The elevator crashed, and I experienced the shock of impact, although I felt no pain because I was momentarily knocked unconscious.

I came to lying face down, unable to move. The lift appeared to be rising slowly, and the door automatically opened. People were gathered outside (I later found out that the crash had been heard all over the building), and I was carried out to an ambulance and taken to a hospital.

***My life from that moment on was never the same.***

Recovery was a slow, painful, and uncomfortable process. Whereas before I had been active in sports, working out at the gym, running, keeping fit, and so on, I was now unable to stand up. My knees had been compressed and couldn't support my body weight; I had to wear a large, uncomfortable orthopedic collar around my neck because my neck had been fractured and could no longer support the weight of my head. My lower back was crushed. My jaw was still sore from the impact, but if I hadn't stuffed the handkerchief in my mouth, I would most certainly have chopped my tongue off with my teeth as, at the moment of impact, the lower jaw smashed into the upper jaw. I realized that if I hadn't gone into a crouch to absorb the shock through the body, I would have been killed by the fracture of my spine. How I knew exactly what actions to take was an intriguing mystery. It wasn't as if I had an emergency contingency plan for elevator crashes.

Over the following months, I was in a lot of pain and experienced great feelings of despondency, resentment, and bitterness. I became vacant, absent from life, and I occupied myself by sitting down and looking out the window. I remember spending entire days gazing out during the autumn, watching leaves fall from the trees, studying the patterns they made, observing how they were rustled and blown about by the wind to form new patterns.

Of course, other things were going on as well. I was being seen by top-notch doctors and receiving all the other benefits that my company medical insurance provided. But the prognosis was always the same: "Sorry, nothing we can do. It will take time."

During these difficult months, a friend suggested that I see an alternative healer. I thought, "Why not? I have nothing else to do!" The sessions I had with this therapist were pleasant, and I found them to be relaxing and helpful. The therapist used a mixture of bodywork, massage, and energy healing. This went on for a few months, until one day, as I was lying on his massage couch, an unusual glaze came into his eyes, and he began speaking in a noticeably different voice. He had suffered from a stroke, and his speech since that event had been slurred, but this time it was eloquent and sonorous. He asked, "Howard, do you want to become well again?"

I was stunned by this question and somehow couldn't get an answer. I had to struggle with it: Do I really want to get well? Finally, after what seemed like a long time, I replied, "Yes, I do want to." I realized that I had become used to being feeble and embittered, and had not even considered that I would really recover. Then, still in this unusual, calm voice, he said, "Howard, forgive all the people that you blame for the accident." "OK," I thought, "I can do this," so I closed my eyes, gathered myself, concentrated with all the force I could muster, and said, "I forgive all those people that I blame for the accident." At that exact moment, it felt as if a great heavy mountain started to lift from me. I felt light, even weightless. I only became aware of this massive weight on me as it dissipated. It was an incredible experience.

When I looked back at him, the glaze from his eyes had gone, and he looked confused. "What happened?" he asked. "Something came over me, and I don't understand it." I told him what had taken place; I was baffled and concerned that he didn't remember. This was definitely a bit weird! Nevertheless, I felt so much different, uplifted and clearer.

Over the next week in this excited and elated state, I of course overexerted myself and subsequently strained my body, and it was back to lying down in bed to recover. As I lay resting, I placed my hands on my chest for comfort, and within seconds, waves of sensation pulsed and washed through me, and the pain went away. The next day, I was again in pain, lying down, and the same thing happened. This went on for about a week, and then it dawned on me that when I placed my hands on my body, the pain disappeared like it was being flushed away.

Immediately following this realization, I felt a kind of "fuzziness" around me, extending about six inches from my body. It was not unlike a low electric current. I could also see iridescent, translucent streamers emanating from my fingers when I touched this field of fuzziness. I started to experiment and found that this invisible fuzziness was around everything. It could be touched and was malleable. I used to make up balls of this electric fuzziness and play ping pong, bouncing it off the ceiling and walls, catching it and throwing it again. Apart from these small and entertaining diversions, the most important matter was that I was making real progress; I could feel that I was getting well. The pain was considerably easier, and my back was becoming increasingly more flexible. The hardness in my back progressively changed from feeling like a heavy slab of concrete to that of a softer and more yielding material. Bit by bit, I could increasingly move my back and bend down, and I didn't need to wear the collar anymore. Even my knees could bend, and I was overjoyed at achieving the ability to walk up a slope. I felt so damn good!

During this period of healing, I experienced some unusual encounters. I remember one night lying in bed asleep, and I kept on hearing a voice whispering repeatedly, "Howard, wake up, wake up," directly into my ear. I woke up and there in front of me was something like an illuminated cinema screen floating in the air. As my eyes focused on the "screen," I could see a group of Tibetan monks dressed in red and saffron robes smiling and enthusiastically waving at me. I was amazed by this wonderful vision, and I really enjoyed it. Then the voice spoke again: "Watch carefully. This is what you have to do, and we will show you exercises that will help your back to get well." Then the scene changed, and the Tibetan monks all lay on their backs and showed me a set of exercises to get my injured back healed. When this was done, they gathered again and with beautiful and warming smiles gently waved goodbye. The floating screen faded away and disappeared. Needless to say, I followed their instructions, and they really helped.

It took two years before I could really resume my life, go back to work, and generally get out and about. In the meantime, I helped a friend with his chronic back pain. I found that I was able to work with this fuzzy field to release pain, very much like I had done with myself. Gradually, through word of mouth, people started to see me for healing. It was an unusual experience because as I focused on the person, I experienced a sense of uplifting and heightened awareness, and I found that as I held an image of the person in my thoughts and saw that individual becoming well, strong, and healthy again, the person experienced a positive reaction. If a person who had a bad back came to me, I would visualize the back becoming strong, firm, straight, and supple, and without a single word taking place between us, the person's back would kind of "unroll" and become straight. I didn't understand the mechanism at work or what was going on, but I did have a strong desire to find out more, so I decided to explore this strange "thing" that was going on within and around me. I used the term *thing* because at that stage I had no understanding of what was happening to me. All I knew was that it worked.

During this transient developmental period, all kinds of unexpected phenomena took place. I became increasingly more conscious of the field of energy around me, and one day I became aware of what I can only describe as a thick steel band clamped around my forehead. The more I focused on it, the more it constricted. It felt alive. The pressure around my head became so tight that my forehead began to ache. I knew that I had to remove whatever was causing the constriction. It took about an hour of intense concentration, and I was sweating so hard that it felt like physical exertion, but gradually I was able to weaken the metal-like band, particle by particle, and get leverage, and then slowly, very slowly, I wrenched the clamp off my forehead.

As soon as this was released, the room filled with dazzling, flashing sparks of color. Colors blazed everywhere; the whole room vibrated and shimmered with stunning hues. The experience was so intense that I had to go outside and walk to the local park to get some air. However, as I moved, this luminescent vision grew even more vivid. I could see pulsating, radiant flecks dancing around people, but this flow of color was not only around people; when I arrived at the park and looked at the trees, I saw an iridescent glow surrounding them. I was totally mesmerized by this astounding experience, and after spending some time wandering around the park, enjoying this exciting display, I made my way home. When I arrived at my house and sat down, I saw a beautiful, scintillating, glowing pink cloud. This pink cloud approached me, and I heard soft, gentle words inside my head that said, "Peace." I felt a glow of warmth and happiness, and the pink cloud gently flowed into me. I had never felt such warmth, friendship, and love. Love cascaded and streamed through and around me, reaching out far beyond. The only way I can describe it is as if I had been touched by an angelic presence.

After all this, my perception expanded in new directions. When I looked at a person, I saw shapes and forms around them. When a person came to me for healing, I saw animals around them. These animals could communicate with me. Sometimes they showed me images, and at other times I would hear their words whispering in my ear. They would tell me about the person, the cause of the illness, and the practice or medicine that would be helpful to that individual. At times I felt that I was becoming very unbalanced, even crazy, yet what kept me on the ground and held me together was the fact that it worked. I had absolutely no frame of reference to explain what was happening to me.

I also started to encounter the darker negative forces that abound. One episode that has stayed in my mind concerns an old friend with whom I had been out of contact for many years. For the sake of anonymity, I'll refer to him as "John." He asked me to help him with his severe migraine headaches. The migraine attacks were so vicious that he was often laid low for days on end. It is relevant to note that he had become a heavy cocaine user and had gone into dealing as a way to finance his habit. One day we sat down together to work on his migraine. Just as I started to move into the receptive, meditative visionary space, I was suddenly punched hard on my forehead. The force knocked me off my stool, and I fell onto the floor. I didn't see it coming, and I asked John, "Why did you do that?" He looked at me in total surprise and said, "I didn't do anything." I felt very unsettled and disturbed by what had happened. My forehead was sore, and in the mirror I could see bruising coming up at the location where I had been struck. I told John that I needed to rest and that we could follow up at another time. I asked him to leave. As soon as he went, I had to lie down. I felt extremely weak and unwell. This situation got worse day by day, and I felt that I was fading away; I had no energy and it was a struggle to get up. Doing basic everyday chores was exhausting. I was listless and depleted of energy.

After a few days of this fatigue, I again brought all my focus and attention into my body. In my mind, I saw every organ, every gland, and every system in my body become alive and pulse with energy. After doing this for hours, I needed a break and went downstairs to make a cup of tea. As I was sitting down, I felt a strange feeling, a kind of vibrating "murmuring" sensation at the base of my spine that grew and grew in intensity. Suddenly it was like a volcanic explosion, with red-hot lava shooting up along my spine and then all through my body. I couldn't move; it was if I was paralyzed, glued to the chair. I could see and feel waves and bands of light swirl around me. This continued until late at night, when suddenly, with a mighty whooshing noise, all this hot lavalike energy shot out the soles of my feet and into the ground with such force that my legs were thrown up in the air. I had been purged of every trace of the junk that had been punched into me. The kundalini energy at the base of my spine had erupted. As soon as this purging was complete, the glowing pink cloud appeared again and flew back into me through my forehead. I felt fully restored and again had that deep experience of bliss and love. A force outside of my conscious self had intervened and saved my ass. I knew then that it was not John who had attacked me but something with him, or more precisely, something put on him.

As I sat down to reflect on this, a strange apparition materialized in the room. It had the appearance of a snake with the head of a lion. The snake came closer and paused in front of me. I knew that this was an ally, a helper, a protector, and, most important of all, a friend. I didn't know how I knew this; I just felt it. I reached out and stroked the furry lion mane, and it spoke to me, saying that it was a guardian and necessary for the work I was doing. I realized that I needed all the help I could get!

Well, back to this "thing" with John. A couple of days later, he called me and asked again if I could help him with his migraine. We arranged a time, and he came around. He sat down on the chair, and I looked at him, but this time with considerably more wariness, and I saw what appeared to be a steaming pile of excrement on top of his head. As I continued to study this, I saw sparks and tendrils of light being drawn from him into this pile of excrement; this "thing" was feeding off him. Gingerly I extended my hands and lifted this putrid substance off his head. This substance felt very slimy and repugnant, and I put it on the floor and quickly stepped back. Instantly it grew into a shadowy amorphous mass towering above me. I was very alarmed by this and didn't know what to do. I felt great apprehension, and then I remembered the lion-headed snake that had been recently introduced to me, so I called this guardian to help me.

There was a blinding flash, and the dark, shapeless mass vanished. All that remained was the pungent odor of sulfur and burnt meat. John was looking at me very strangely; he said he saw a flash of light and asked where the smell was coming from. I told him what had happened and made it clear this obscene thing had been drawn to him by his use of cocaine. He looked so different. His face had become younger, with the lines smoothed out, and his expression glowed. He was delighted that the migraine headache had vanished. I suggested that he look at himself in the mirror, which he did, and he returned with a great big grin on his face.

John, unfortunately, did not stop or reduce his cocaine usage, and a few months later the migraines returned with a vengeance. He contacted me and asked for help. I treated him again, albeit with a lot more awareness on my part, and this relieved him, but this cycle didn't end, and I regretfully realized that unless he made the decision to stop, all the time and effort would be fruitless. I also didn't appreciate having this nauseating, obnoxious mess brought into my house. I saw John again a couple of times over the next months, and he had changed. He looked as if he was being consumed. His face was drawn, and he had lost a lot of weight. He had a very negative and aggressive attitude, and there was no way I could reach him or offer any support. It was time to break contact, which I did, and over the next few days he left sinister messages on my answering machine. Whatever had got him had him.

The experiences with John had taught me a lot. I clearly saw the effects of hard drug use and extreme negative thoughts in a different way. I became less naive and knew that there were tangible energies out there. Some were benign and helpful, some not so benign. I understood that our practices and attitudes act like magnetic forces, drawing those energies to us, and in turn they are able to influence us. It was an awareness of the "dreamer dreaming the dream and then the dream dreaming the dreamer."

On this theme, and around this time, I had another important teaching, one that I have endeavored to fulfill to this day. It was a direct teaching by these invisible beings. This teaching was not fluffy; it was made difficult due to my innate stubborn streak because I felt like I was being reprogrammed.

I found that if I had a negative or unpleasant thought about a person, my head immediately felt as if it was being crushed in a vise, and it was painful. The pain would stay with me for hours afterward. If, however, I had a positive, enhancing thought about someone, I felt a wonderfully warm glow flush through my body, which left me in a virtual state of bliss.

I knew that these actions were being imposed on me from "outside" of myself, and I absolutely resented this. I saw it as an imposition on my free will; if I want to be unpleasant, that's my business! I confess that I resisted this as much as I could, even though I knew deep within that the purpose was aimed at making me a better person. However much I tried, I couldn't prevent it, and eventually I realized that I had to seriously change my attitude and become aware of the nature of my thoughts. What really upset me most about this whole affair was that it gave my well-developed ego a hell of a bashing. I was being trained by these incorporeal beings or spirits in exactly the same way that a donkey is trained—using the carrot and the stick—except that in this scenario I was the donkey! They certainly have a good sense of humor.

So I sat down and considered a way to resolve this, and I figured out that I had no choice but to discipline my thoughts. I had the notion to place a metaphorical "thought supervisor" in my mind. This supervisor had the appearance of a traditional British policeman in uniform and helmet holding a truncheon. His task was to inspect my thoughts before they were transmitted. This entailed stopping the negative and disharmonious thoughts and transforming them into gentle and gracious thoughts before they were broadcast into the world. As this function started to work, I no longer suffered from the viselike pain. After a period of time, I was no longer even aware of the presence of this "policeman"; positive thinking had become natural and ingrained in me. Even now, when I am really tempted to have an unkind or aggressive thought about a person, I have to dissipate the thought itself and replace it with an amiable or neutral thought. I had figured out that thoughts have power, that they are a form of energy that can influence reality and have an effect on people.

This is not a fallacy by any means, and I'm not proposing anything out of the ordinary here, as you yourself may have had experiences of manifesting in the world what you are thinking, whether positive or negative. The fundamental premise is that our thoughts are vibrational waves that connect to energy on the same wavelength, thus drawing people or events to us that are on a similar wavelength. Although this concept is not scientific per se, there is sufficient anecdotal evidence to suggest not rejecting it out of hand. Subjective events are hard to measure, and one of the greatest challenges of quantum science is explaining the phenomenon of the observer influencing the experiment simply through the act of observing.

I found that another benefit of managing my thoughts was that it stopped me from being reactive in difficult situations and provided an opportunity to be brutally honest with myself as to why I wanted to react and why I felt the way I did. Where did those feelings come from? Often they came from a sense of being hurt or offended by another person. I have learned to understand that the painful emotions are mine—they belong to me—and in fact the other person has done me a service by reflecting back to me my unresolved wounds. If you work with this attitude, it really is a gift, a blessing rather than a violation of some sort.

# 2
# STARTING TO HEAL

*The wound is the place where the Light enters you.*

RUMI

Whenever I hear and read about people's reasons for following a spiritual path, they are often beautiful and inspirational. When I found out my reason for carrying out the healing work, it certainly was different. This revelation happened when a man came to see me. He was a prominent teacher in psychotherapy, and when we met, he clearly appeared unwell: his face was pale, and his movements were shaky. He said that two weeks previously he had given a lecture and that some hostile people in the audience for perverse and malevolent reasons of their own had energetically attacked him. He said that since then he had felt like he was fading away. Every day he felt himself becoming weaker and weaker. As he sat down and I attuned to him, I became aware that he was covered in what looked to me like large putrid leeches. I could say that this was the symbolic form of what was making him weak or that this is how my psyche "read" and interpreted the nature of the entity that was draining his life force.

I started to lift these leechlike things from him. They felt repulsive,

18

repugnant, and obnoxious. I could also smell them, and at times I nearly gagged and threw up. However, I persevered, and when the last one was removed, he looked like a new man. His facial coloring was robust, he stood strong, and he looked well and vibrant. We discussed what had happened, and he resolved to act on his awareness and trust his intuition in these situations.

After he left, I was still feeling a bit queasy from the evening's work. I needed to take a shower to feel clean again. As I stood in the shower, I had the overwhelming urge to vomit, and I threw up all over the shower. I knew it was from clearing the "leeches," and then I questioned my reasons for doing this work. I spoke out loud, "Why the fuck am I doing this?" Then a deep, disembodied voice boomed out of nowhere, echoing around me, and said, "Someone has got to do it!" I had to laugh at that because that was a message I could understand. As I mentioned before, these beings do have a sense of humor.

## I DISCOVER SHAMANISM

I wanted not just to learn more about healing but also to understand the inexplicable phenomena taking place. This led me to getting in touch with a national spiritual healing organization, and I enrolled in the courses. During these studies, I was told that I was approaching this work incorrectly and had to stop the way I did healing. I should follow the official guidelines and work the "proper" way, which was to become a "channel" for divine energies. This required that I place my hands in certain positions on the client's body and raise my energies to the light. I learned various visualizations and practiced healing with the other course participants. I found it interesting and quite pleasant, but somewhere it missed something earthy and fundamental. Anyhow, I had switched off the way I naturally perceived and carried out my work, and now performed healing in the "correct" manner.

During this period, when I was working in the way of the "approved" spiritual healer, I met Leo Rutherford, who was to become a helpful influence, close friend, and eventual colleague. We took to each other immediately and found that there was a great rapport between us. Leo was involved in something called shamanism and had established Eagle's Wing Centre for Contemporary Shamanism in 1983. Leo invited me to join a group of his friends at a sweat lodge ceremony, and I found it a moving and beautiful experience. As we became friendlier, I discussed some of my experiences and said that I felt that I had "invented" this work. No one else I knew could relate to it, and I had no name for it. Leo smiled and with great amusement proceeded to tell me that I hadn't invented this work; it had been around for many thousands of years and was called shamanism! I sighed with relief, and laughed and laughed . . . I really did think at times that I was going off the wall and round the bend! At last a map for understanding my journey, and a deep feeling of having found my home.

I still continued to work in the spiritual healing way, and I recall one day in which I was working with a group of healers and one of the most experienced and authoritative among them asked me to help in healing something (which she referred to as a major block) on a woman's shoulder. My thoughts were, "If she can't do it, what chance have I got?" Then I suddenly knew that I had to go back to my natural way. As I attuned to the woman, I immediately saw a raven sitting on her shoulder. I touched it and started to lift it off. The raven struggled, vigorously twisting and turning this way and that, and tried to fly away just like a physical bird would. I held on to it as tightly as possible while I visualized disassembling its structure until it became a cloud of translucent energy and could be released.

When I turned back to the person, she was in tears, remembering the death of her father, who had been murdered thirty years back. She realized that she had never mourned for him. Once the raven had been lifted from her, she was able to release the pent-up grief and start to mourn. I was amazed and powerfully moved by this experience, yet still for some months after this I maintained the "proper" spiritual way of healing.

Later in the year I attended a fabulous and life-changing event, the annual New Year's Eagle's Wing Shamanic Gathering held at Grimstone Manor, a large mansion situated on extensive grounds, adjacent to one of the last remaining wild places in England, Dartmoor in Devon. The gathering was a powerful and moving experience involving ceremony and all-night trance dancing accompanied by a relay of drummers. We learned about the medicine wheel, enjoyed lots of social interaction, ate good food, and last but not least shared about ourselves in circles. I really felt privileged to witness other participants opening up their inner being and telling others about their problems and the difficulties they had lived through. I found it to be a beautiful and exquisitely cathartic experience.

During one of the sharing circles, a woman spoke of her enduring agony. She sobbed and said she felt like all her life she had had knives in her vagina, and she asked the group if anybody could help her. On hearing this, I immediately felt a bolt of electricity in me, and I knew that I should offer my help, but rather than respond right away, as I felt slightly apprehensive about this, I decided to give it some thought. However, after the circle had closed, Leo approached me and asked if I would help. He had spoken to the woman about me, and she was open to the idea. For the purpose of anonymity, I'll refer to the woman as "Alice." Subsequently, we arranged a time and a place for this.

Alice arrived with Leo and a friend, so we started and she lay down on some cushions. I knew immediately that I had to work in my "old way," and I attuned to her and saw these "knives" suspended above her genital area. I extended my energy and passed my hand a few inches above her body, and the "knives" became loose, began to dissolve, and were then released from her. After this was completed, I noticed what appeared to be an elephant's trunk inserted into her vagina. I held it and gently started to withdraw it, and then I realized that it was not an elephant's trunk after all; it was a massive penis. I reduced the massive penis to a more normal size, and then within moments I was holding a man's "testicles" in my hand. I looked at the man and described him to Alice. She said in a little girl voice, "Daddy."

The man I described was her father, who still possessed her, and I am not saying this figuratively, because when I told him to leave his daughter, he replied, "She is mine." I called upon the incorporeal guides to remove him and take him to a place where he could be helped, and as his energy body was detached from her, there was only what I can describe as an explosive release and a sense of enormous liberation emanating from Alice. This led to an indescribable wave of sadness and anguish from Alice as she remembered the times that her father had sexually abused her. Her friend and I spent time with Alice as her body went through the throes of this release. I remember looking at her face, and it was as if a burden of the ages had been cast off. She looked much younger and more alive. I knew that the massive size of the penis in her energy body was how it must have appeared to her when she was young. How horrific the experience must have been. She smiled and said that she had despaired of ever getting help.

After this, I went for a long walk on the moors. It was a cold but sunny day and unusually luminescent. I walked for what seemed to be miles, climbed to the summit of a tor (a rocky peak), sat down in a place of total silence (always a novel experience for a city dweller), and just looked at the moors from this vantage point. It was then I decided to do this work, in the way that I could, using the gifts that I had. From that moment of commitment in Dartmoor, I have never stopped doing this work, and it has continued to grow and develop.

Later on, as my work grew, I started to understand the interaction of energy bodies and fields generated by thoughts and emotions. I knew by attuning to a client whether another person, or a group of people, was "obsessed" in some way with the client. It was as if their energy filaments were entangled with the client's energy field. Thoughts and emotions (whether expressed or unexpressed) could take on an energy form and a life of their own. It is so critical that we become aware of and take ownership of our negative and diminishing thoughts and feelings. This is the way to start the epic journey to heal ourselves. We have to bring the unexpressed or buried forces within us to the surface.

It was about two weeks after the New Year event that the experience on the moor was reinforced. At home one evening, I had a vision, one so strong that it really felt like I was somehow transported to open countryside. It was a summer's night, and the sky was clear and filled with stars. I saw a lake, the surface smooth and without ripples. The stars were perfectly reflected in the lake's surface, and for a moment it felt as if I was in space surrounded by stars. I was quite overawed by this. I then saw something move, and as I looked more closely, I saw a Native American man beckoning to me. As soon as he knew I had seen him, he turned around and started walking downhill. He turned around as if to see if I was following him. He then paused and pointed with his arm to a village below the hill. We walked together in silence into the village.

He led me to a circular lodge and indicated that I should enter by opening the door flap. I went inside; it was pitch dark, and I couldn't see a thing except for a red glow. I waited until my eyes became adjusted to the dark, and then I could see the glow was coming from a pipe bowl. Shortly after that I began to discern an old Native American man with white hair smoking the pipe. I approached him, he indicated that I should sit down, and then he passed his pipe to me. I smoked the pipe in silence for a little while, and then returned it to him. He said, "Your work is to bring back the old teachings and ways into modern times." I was stunned by this and didn't know how to respond. I'm sure that I should have had lots of questions, but if I had I certainly could not get it together to ask any of them. I simply said thank you and got up to leave. He smiled at me and said goodbye. I wanted to give him something as a gift, and I looked in my pockets, but I had nothing with me. He found this amusing and smiled at me.

When I left the lodge, the man outside was waiting for me, and we went back up the hill away from the village. My mind whirled. I felt as if I was twisting and spinning around, and then I found myself back in my room. At times, I have reflected on this remarkable experience, and it has helped me in those times of doubt. At the time I did not know what had happened, but later I came to understand that this was an excursion into magical reality.

Other challenging encounters occurred, and to be honest I was not prepared to talk about them for a very long time, as they would be regarded as very wacky indeed. It's only now that I feel a tad more comfortable that I can write about them. I went through what people could call an alien abduction experience.

To set the context, this happened after I returned from a journey to Egypt in 1991. I was privileged to have the opportunity to visit the Great Pyramid at dawn, well before the official opening time, and it was an incredible experience. As I entered the King's Chamber, the energy that met me was overwhelmingly intense. This crystalline energy was so dense* that it felt as if I could cut it with a knife. I positioned myself in the massive pink granite sarcophagus, and in there the crystalline energy was even more concentrated; I fell immediately into a deep visionary trance. In these visions I saw eight-foot-tall blue-skinned bipedal beings ascending and descending along the pyramid. I understood that the pyramid at its zenith was some form of interdimensional gateway, or stargate.

Even after I returned home to London, this unreal connection was present. I wasn't abducted in the literal sense of being physically taken into an extraterrestrial craft, but every evening when I was alone, I felt strong presences near me. They would appear to me as the same blue-skinned beings I had encountered in the King's Chamber. They induced me to become drowsy and then sleep, and during this sleep, they made modifications on me. These operations, as I call them, were initially painful and uncomfortable. It felt like an apparatus was being inserted and implanted in my head, in particular into my right frontal lobe, and of course it was damned inconvenient too. I could be put

---

*Likely due to the high quartz content of the granite and the geometric symmetry.

to sleep while eating my evening dinner and come to later with food smeared on my face and hair because my head had been lying in the dinner plate.

I remember writhing and rolling around the floor in pain at times as these things were being implanted in me. I couldn't stop these procedures from taking place because I was made so drowsy. Eventually I learned to negotiate with the incorporeal beings: "Let me finish my dinner first, and then I'll go and lie down." It wasn't much of a negotiation, but it made it easier. These changes went on for a couple of months, and over this period the invisible implants—which felt like they were sticking outside of my head—gradually faded away and somehow integrated into my head, which felt a lot better.

After the modifications had stopped, I clearly knew what the effects were: a heightened sensitivity and receptivity to people's thoughts, along with an understanding of the influences and circumstances surrounding them. One day while walking through a London shopping mall, I was musing on these alterations, and I thought to myself, "It looks like I will have to trust these buggers." A loud bass voice boomed out, "No, it is we who have to trust you!" I was a bit shaken up by this and didn't like the idea of what I had got into. Just who were these bloody spirits, telling me what to do? Giving me responsibilities, and knowing what I was thinking! I didn't like it one bit! But it brought matters into much more focus, and I approached things in a less casual way after that. I did find the heightened level of sensitivity unsettling, but I found that I could switch it off and on, so to speak. This is really necessary because it is possible to become very ungrounded and spaced out if you don't switch it off when you aren't using it.

Michael Harner, who founded the Foundation for Shamanic Studies, relates a story that took place in the 1960s, when he was a young anthropologist working in the Amazon with the Jivaro people. He said that a man in the village wandered around talking to the trees and staring into space and acting in a generally mysterious manner. Michael asked his guide, "Is this man your shaman?" The guide answered by pointing to his head, wiggling his finger, and saying, "No, el esta loco."[1] That is a useful anecdote and good to keep in mind because the role of a shaman is to be grounded and yet be able to at will enter into an altered state of consciousness in order to commune with the ineffable, the noncorporeal domain of spirit.

# 3

# MAPS OF REALITY

*Reality leaves a lot to the imagination.*

JOHN LENNON

Nonordinary, or alternative, reality is a subject that needs to be examined even though it fits the definitions of *ambiguity* and *ineffability*. The age-old question is where is this "place" that people who practice shamanic journeying go? Most certainly it is not in our familiar everyday physical reality. Where, then, could it exist? Perhaps reality itself is much more complicated than we thought. The latest mind-stretching research by scientists exploring the quantum universe points a finger at the concept of a universe that not only is infinite but also is increasing at an ever-accelerating velocity. If that is not cosmic enough, they are hinting at the theoretical possibility that there are also an infinite number of multidimensional universes that are also infinite in size and expanding at an ever-increasing velocity.

I've spent quite a few hours sitting outdoors under a tree in the anticipation that something like Newton's apple would fall down and provide a flash of inspiration, but the more I attempt to fathom this concept, the more my mind gets tangled at an ever-increasing velocity. Endeavoring to comprehend a cohesive cosmic awareness has been the ultimate "holy grail" quest for philosophers, sages, and wise men and women for millennia. Magnificent minds such as those of David Bohm, Krishnamurti, Alan Watts, Timothy Leary, Terence McKenna, Joseph Campbell, and Albert Einstein have put forward insightful, enlightened, and in some cases proven explanations for this immense space-time, cosmic Weltanschauung, or worldview.

One of the most interesting facets of this subject is that shamans and sages since antiquity have been contemplating a hidden or multidimensional reality. A vast body of experiential knowledge and insight from spiritual traditions suggests that a sublime universal energy exists that can be accessed from within us, and just as we use maps to navigate, these traditions have produced maps so that we too can navigate in this other reality. A traditional map of alternate reality further developed by the neoshamanic movement describes three discrete regions or levels: the upper world, the lower world, and the middle world. Each world has different characteristics and contains sources of wisdom that a shaman accesses via an altered state of consciousness and, importantly, brings back into our physical reality, often for purposes of healing, divination, or a collective need.

The Romanian mythologist and philosopher Mircea Eliade in his book *Shamanism: Archaic Techniques of Ecstasy* presents a crosscultural comparison of shamanic cultures all over the globe. One notion central to many cultures is the concept of an *axis mundi,* also called the cosmic axis, world mountain, or world tree. It is the precise center of the connection between the world and the celestial realms. Eliade proposes that shamanic cultures have much in common and that any differences are typically due to variances in climate, geography, and local environment. From this a reader might assume that a shaman practicing in the hot and humid Amazon rainforest could visit a shaman practicing in the frozen steppes of Siberia, and each would understand what the other was doing. In effect, they are singing the same song; the words are simply different.

Even though Eliade's work on shamanism has been incredibly influential on the practice of neoshamanism, I disagree with his broad generalizations based on my own field observations and a huge body of studies on anthropology and ethnobotany made available in recent years. Eliade describes the shamanic tradition of communing with hallucinogenic plants as a degenerative form of shamanic practice, one that stands in opposition to his theory of shamanism, which is the celestial ascent of a shaman and out-of-the-body journeys to the spirit realms. One must bear in mind that he was an academic rather than an experiential anthropologist. To quote Steve Beyer, author of *Singing to the Plants*, "It is important to note that Eliade never met a shaman, never lived in an indigenous culture where shamans practiced, and never observed a shamanic ceremony. Everything he knew about the topic of his book he learned from the writings of others."[1]

In my own travels I've worked with shamans who have spent many years in apprenticeship, with a large part of that time spent living alone in the rainforest dieting on the plants and deepening their connection with the spirits. (When dieting on a particular plant, the consciousness of the shaman and the plant meet. Using this technique, shamans learn the medicinal properties and other pertinent attributes, and more important, develop a magical affinity with the plant.) From a cultural perspective their shamanic credentials are impeccable. Yet none would fall into Eliade's *specific* definition of a shaman, as distinct from a medicine man or woman, sorcerer, healer, diviner, magician, or herbalist. His specific definition is: "the shaman specializes in a trance during which his soul is believed to leave his body and ascend to the sky or descend to the underworld."[2] Many of the shamans that I have worked with do not travel to one of three separate realms, the upper, middle, and lower worlds, nor do they harbor the notion of an axis mundi.

Even so, Eliade's conclusions have played a major part in the practice of contemporary shamanism in the West. His work has given great impetus to the cross-cultural aspects of the neoshamanic movement. Michael Harner has created an impressive and influential body of work that draws upon this all-inclusive concept of shamanism, termed *core shamanism*. This has developed into a Westernized composite of various shamanic practices, forming a very accessible and powerful form of shamanism for the modern Western world.

It is particularly interesting to explore how the three shamanic realms are represented in cultures around the globe. In the East, for instance, the ancient Chinese and Tibetan pantheon is depicted in paintings and *thangkas* (a traditional Tibetan Buddhist silk painting) as residing in concentric worlds within worlds. Each world is separated by the sky and clouds, and each world includes rivers, mountains, trees, dwellings, and so on. These paintings can be regarded as maps of the culture's multidimensional reality. These maps are specific, depicting the locations of where the gods, the ancestors, and the teachers lived, and can be used like guidebooks for navigating through multidimensional reality, or the spirit worlds. The ultimate expression of this type of document, in my view, is the *Tibetan Book of the Dead,* with its detailed descriptions of the passage through the *bardo.* In Tibetan Buddhism, consciousness (and therefore life) is a continuum, and the bardo is a form of existence between incarnations on Earth. The *Tibetan Book of the Dead,* therefore, is a chart to assist the individual consciousness to find its way through the experience of reality between incarnations.

As we move farther west, into Siberia, the structure, or the interpretation of the structure, changes. In the upper world reside the gods who created the universe, the stars, the sun, and the planet. These distant gods have little time and little interest in the affairs of humans—they are simply too busy running the universe—so any individuals making supplications to them had better be patient. The lower world, however, houses the gods who created life on Earth, the plants, the animals, and the humans. Here the gods have much more interest in people. The lower world is viewed as a place of sustenance and nourishment; it was the Mother.

When you get to our modern Western society, and yes we still have these three worlds, their names are very familiar to us. They are called heaven, Earth, and hell. The problem here is that the lower world has become demonized and is considered a very bad place, where all the sinners (disobedient people) go to suffer eternal damnation, hellfire, and other terrible punishments. From a shamanic and a psychological perspective, this has created the major problem of separation. By demonizing the lower world, the place that holds the feminine qualities of nurturing and sustenance, our society has become disconnected from these attributes. The story of the Garden of Eden, also known as the "Fall of Man," exemplifies this separation. We can see the effects that this fundamental myth has caused historically in Western society. From the outset, women are depicted as bad, and the feminine principle is condemned. Eve, the first woman, is tempted by the Devil, and she in turn encourages Adam to eat the fruit of the forbidden Tree of Knowledge. Thus, it comes to pass that we sinners (humans) are unceremoniously escorted out of this biblical utopia by the angelic bouncers brandishing fiery swords! The idea that we are rejected by God, advanced by the loathsome doctrine of original sin, has had tragic consequences in our world.

We have the potential to live in paradise; this planet Earth nurtures and loves us unconditionally. We are born of it, and we are her children. From this source we receive food, shelter, water, and everything else we could possibly need to live. We enjoy lives of creativity and beauty, and explore the consciousness of ourselves and the Earth. There is enough for everybody.

Historically, Western society has lived by an anthropocentric view of our universe in which our planet and thus we humans reside at the center. In 1633, at his trial for heresy, the Italian physicist and astronomer Galileo was forced to recant (under threat of torture by the Holy Inquisition) his published statement that the Earth revolves around the sun and not the other way around, as per the dogma and science of the day. This trial resulted in Galileo being sentenced to life imprisonment. Today, this still stands as a powerful symbol of the struggle for the freedom of inquiry against the established authority. We explore this theme in the arts, such as Bertolt Brecht's play *Life of Galileo*. Eventually, in 1979, Pope John Paul II opened an investigation into the astronomer's condemnation, calling for its reversal, and in 1992 a papal commission acknowledged the Vatican's error, which was undeniably graceful of them. . . . The wheels of justice do indeed turn slowly.

In contemporary Western psychology, nonordinary, or alternate, reality is not seen as an *external* place located somewhere in a multidimensional cosmos; rather, it is considered to be an extension of our inner psyche. When an individual does "inner work" and connects to a higher level of wisdom and awareness, it is regarded as linking to a collective consciousness or to archetypes. In my view, this perspective is not in disagreement with the shamanic outlook. Both views are valid; it is only a question of the standpoint.

From another source, far away from civilization, so to speak, deep in the Amazon rainforest, we find the quintessential wisdom of my teacher and dear friend Pablo Amaringo, who depicted this alchemic process as a metaphor *within a metaphor* in his paintings. In the extract from the painting *Concentración Palistica,* shown in color plate 1, the hierarchy of grades of shaman is symbolized by the winged vessels with fires burning in them. Going from bottom to top, the Onaya, Banco Puma, Muraya, Sumiruna, and Banco Sumi are represented (the Banco Sumi is the highest grade achievable). The winged vessels symbolize that those who embark on the path of learning from ayahuasca are all moving toward higher levels of knowledge and wisdom. Pablo also saw this hierarchy of grades as a metaphor for the evolving consciousness of humanity. Note: The full painting with a detailed explanatory narrative is available in the book *The Ayahuasca Visions of Pablo Amaringo.*

So is there an alternate reality that coexists side by side with our physical reality? Is our perception of time—that it is linear and sequential, similar to a river flowing into the future—the whole picture? In my experience, the world we perceive through our physical senses is a projection of this unseen reality. Our perception of the world, although received through our sensory systems, is shaped by our culture and language. In recent years metaphysics and science have investigated and attempted to understand and explain how the nonphysical aspects of reality function.

Also, the lens through which we perceive time is illusory. It is as if there is one moment in time, one vast ever-moving moment, in which anything that has ever happened is somewhere still happening. There is an ongoing convergence in our view of reality from the ancient esoteric traditions and modern quantum physics. In some respects, quantum physics is now pointing in the same direction as the ancient shamans and sages have pointed for fifty thousand years. For example, *The End of Time,* a book by the eminent British physicist Julian Barbour, challenges the most fundamental conventions in scientific understanding. Barbour proposes that we live in a universe that has neither past nor future. We inhabit a strange new world in which we are both alive and dead in the same instant. In this eternal present, our sense of the passage of time is nothing more than a giant cosmic illusion. This other dimension, presented by Barbour, this single, vast, ever-moving moment in time, which has been experienced and expressed by indigenous people since antiquity, often called the spirit world, has been eloquently described by Black Elk, the Oglala Lakota holy man and great visionary, as

the world where there is nothing but the spirits of all things. This is the real world that is behind this one, and everything we see here is something like a shadow from that world.[3]

In the words of the celebrated Mazatec shaman Maria Sabina (documented by R. Gordon Wasson):

> There is a world beyond ours, a world that is far away, nearby and invisible. And there is where God lives, where the dead live, the spirits and the saints, a world where everything has already happened and everything is known. That world talks. It has a language of its own. I report what it says.[4]

My experience has shown me that we individuals are not projecting a field of collective archetypes; rather, we are the projection of the universal field, or energetic matrix. The physical world we experience is but the perception of our physical senses rather than an absolute fact. I refer to this expanded inclusive reality as the Great Domain.

Carlos Castaneda in his books describes the act of *stopping the world*. Of course he doesn't mean that the physical world stops, but rather our experience of the world stops for a moment when we have an experience that defies conventional understanding. Such an event challenges us to change our way of seeing, going beyond the physical world and thereby expanding our consciousness. My accident in the elevator was just such a moment. Sometimes this phenomenon happens (typically when we least expect it) in the most mundane circumstances. One memorable occurrence for me was when I was walking along a busy road in London. I was dwelling in my thoughts about the Jivaro people and their relation to the physical world, a world they experience as "not the real world," more of an illusion. Anyway, I was walking in meditative rhythm, thinking, "What would it be like to see and live in the world in this way?" when suddenly the world around me started to shimmer and disappear. Buildings became phantomlike, the ground started to fade away, and I was so incredibly startled that I immediately snapped out of the experience, back into an everyday state of consciousness. It was just a micromoment but a significant eye opener.

One of the most philosophical and inspirational teachings that I have received from the spirit guides took place during a deep meditation in a period when I was feeling sad following a personal loss. This was a poetic articulation regarding the nature of existence and reality. It expresses a reality that defies rational explanation.

*There was a time before creation when thought had no focus or being. Thought was like a breeze uncontained, unwilling to be tamed. From everywhere, thought drew itself to a central point, changing from something random and developing an experience of structure. When this structure was formed and completed, the genetics of the universe were in place. This structure provides a means by which God can be recognized within us.*

*From this point forward, when structure could be developed no further, when thought and experience had become one, the structure expanded within itself and thus became creation. Creation follows structure; it is therefore useless to imagine that one can create anything of worth or value from outside that structure. That structure is continually expanding outward from itself, like a stretched snowflake, creating patterns that would be, if we could see them, a delight to the eye. Why should it be important to know that what we call flow is the movement of creation, that the desire to fill infinite space with creation is the reason for our existence? Just as the human body has a genetic makeup, the universe has an underlying structure, a form predestined and predecided, in that initial act of creation.*

*Just as atoms are ruled by physical laws, we are subject to the rules of that structure, that will of creation. The structure laid down in that initial state of creation allows us to transcend the human form and its apparent limitations.*

*Those limitations are merely beliefs; accepting as true those things you call human, physical, and frail, which separate you from the oneness and the connectedness that you so desire.*

*In the not-so-distant past, it took time to elevate one's mind to the awareness of that initial state of creation. Now it is possible to integrate the understanding of that state and make it your state for healing.*

*The energy of love is the energy of the initial act of creation. There is not one atom, one form or thought or intention or understanding, that is not affected by this movement outward from the central point. One can see and understand, hold and embrace the reason for existence as part of that initial state. It is pointless to consider a state of enlightenment, for within this exchange you are the reason for existence, you are enlightenment, at one with the light, and you can be nothing else than enlightened. This word, this vibration, is a statement, a recognition of the oneness of the self with that initial state of creation. It means nothing more and nothing less.*

*Look at an ocean. How does it exist as an ocean? It is formed of many droplets, which are themselves formed by many atoms working in harmony with each other to create an illusion of the whole. Each atom exists in its own right, and the space in between holds that atom as an atom. It is in that space in between that we find the light, the memory of the initial structure of creation, the master plan of creation, and you are now within that space and also contained in that space, a vessel and the water that fills it. Simply be aware of this.*

*This is how you exist, this is why you exist, and this is how you understand your reason for existence from being in this space.*

What impels our innate desire to develop an awareness of and to explore the invisible alternate realties? Well, apart from the basic human drive to gain knowledge and understand the universe we inhabit, we should seriously consider that there is also a biological, a social, and a spiritual need for us to explore the alternate realities. In the many hundreds of thousands of years of human evolution, we have developed the faculties and the neurochemistry that precisely allow us to perceive and relate beyond the physical world.

Knowledge of these inner transcendent states has been integral to the extraordinary human sojourn on the planet. Our ancestors knew how to stimulate the human organism to shift into these expanded states of awareness, or trance states, to explore the alternate dimensions of reality. The rhythmic beat of the drum, the rhythmic flow of the dance and chanting are invoked universally to awaken our remarkable ability to enter these states of consciousness. Here science can provide insight. At 200 to 220 pulses (beats) per minute, the brain changes its neurological state, and high levels of beta endorphins and neurotransmitters such as serotonin are synthesized, resulting in the activation of a very different brain pattern, specifically the *theta* pattern. This brain wave relates to spatial awareness, creative thought, and the relaxed dream state in which we can access our deepest memories, spiritual connections, and sources of inspiration. This neatly dovetails with the traditional shamanic cultures that work with the rhythm of the drum or rattle to induce altered states.

Because Western society provides no structure to support and help people reach the theta brain state, they are suffering what anthropologist Felicitas Goodman defines as *ecstasy deprivation*. The lack of trance work and expanded states of awareness have become the norm in Western society, in her view, with serious consequences. Not only are our natural biological and primal needs not supported, but some Westerners try to compensate for this deprivation with high levels of alcohol and drug abuse.

In some cultures, psychotropic plants are used to move beyond the limitations of the physical world and into other realities. We have been conditioned to view this as a primitive or backward tradition, but it lies at the heart of Western culture as well. Benny Shanon, professor of cognitive psychology at the Hebrew University of Jerusalem, wrote an article "Biblical Entheogens: A Speculative Hypothesis" in *Time and Mind: The Journal of Archaeology, Consciousness, and Culture*.

> As far as Moses on Mount Sinai is concerned, it was either a supernatural cosmic event, which I don't believe, or a legend, which I don't believe either, or finally, and this is very probable, an event that joined Moses and the people of Israel under the effect of narcotics.[5]

The worldwide media interest in Benny Shanon's paper about Moses and entheogens is encouraging us to take a good and hard look at the roots of religions. Some theorize that religions grew out of fertility cults and that participants made use of shamanic practices such as entheogenic plants to bring about a spiritual communion with the universal consciousness, or the mind of God.

It's important to note that Shanon compares the psychotropic effects of ayahuasca to those produced by concoctions made from the bark of the acacia tree, which is frequently mentioned in the Bible.

Acacias contain a number of alkaloids that have a profound hallucinogenic effect on humans, including dimethyltryptamine (DMT). The leaves and stems are brewed together with an effective monoamine oxidase inhibitor (MAOI) containing plant, typically Syrian rue (*Peganum harmala*), which also grows in the region (southern Israel and the Sinai Peninsula). This brew is taken orally, similar to the Amazonian brew ayahuasca, which is also a combination of at least two plants, typically the leaves of the *chacruna* plant (*Psychotria viridis*), which contains the vision-inducing alkaloids (DMT), and the ayahuasca vine itself (*Banisteriopsis caapi*), which acts as an inhibitor (MAOI) to prevent the body's enzymes from neutralizing the tryptamine alkaloids. This is known as the MAOI effect, which was discovered by Western science in the 1950s, even though it has been known for thousands of years by our ancestors. This biochemical reaction forms the working basis for an entire class of antidepressant SSRI (selective serotonin reuptake inhibitor) pharmaceutical products such as Prozac and Seroxat.

According to *Easton's Bible Dictionary,* the acacia tree may very well be the "burning bush" (Exodus 3:2) that Moses encountered in the desert. Also, in the Christian tradition, Christ's crown of thorns was woven from acacia. It is of great interest and significance that the humble acacia is so prominent in these two biblical narratives. These narratives have formed the nucleus of these religions and shaped the destiny of hundreds of millions of people. I know it is only speculation, but to me these could be more than just references to an available wood; these could be allegorical or coded references to a plant providing an entheogenic experience, which lies at the heart of religions, as Dr. Shanon conjectures. It is a thought-provoking matter that in Exodus 37 God gave clear instructions to Moses specifying that acacia wood was to be used for the Ark, the Table, and the Altar. These artifacts were looted by the Romans under the command of Titus, the son of the Emperor Vespasian, at the sack and destruction of Jerusalem in 70 CE. The mystery of the whereabouts of the Ark still captures the popular imagination in our culture, as *Raiders of the Lost Ark* demonstrates.

Is that a coincidence or is it an allusion to sacramental use of entheogens?

John Allegro, in his book *The Sacred Mushroom and the Cross: A Study of the Nature and Origins of Christianity within the Fertility Cults of the Ancient Near East,* postulates, based on the etymology of words and the development of language, that the religions emanating from the Middle East were based on fertility cults and entheogens.

Allegro's theory is visionary and groundbreaking. He was the first to propose in some detail that two major religions—Christianity and, by extension, Judaism—were traditionally entheogen-oriented and that the entheogen was *Amanita muscaria,* commonly known as the fly agaric mushroom or fly amanita. His book was published at a time when there was little to no awareness of the use of entheogens, and it was indeed a courageous act to publish the book. Unfortunately, he was metaphorically crucified for his ideas.* Meanwhile, the argument that Jesus was not an actual person but an anthropomorphized hallucinogenic mushroom rolls on and on.

Earlier I discussed the traditional three worlds cosmology; let's not

---

*Back in the 1960s the outraged reaction against these ideas was so strong that it destroyed Allegro's career. The book was not published in the United Kingdom because it was regarded as blasphemous, and blasphemy was still a crime. Finally, in 2008, this archaic law was scrapped in England.

conclude that this is an obsolescent concept. This archaic tenet is still alive and kicking in our Western society, in fact it is dogma for millions of people. In the current adaption of the three worlds, the upper world has been renamed as "heaven" and the lower world has also received a totally new designation and role, becoming "hell." In this revision, the middle world is our physical world, the Earth. So plus ça change!

# 4
# THE SHAMANIC JOURNEY
## Awakening the Dream Body

*Whither will my path yet lead me? This path is stupid, it goes in spirals, perhaps in circles, but whichever way it goes, I will follow it.*

HERMANN HESSE, *SIDDHARTHA*

Shamanism has always been a pragmatic system. It utilizes time-tested methods and tools that enable us to directly access the world of sprit, the place of causality. Shamanism employs no priests, hierarchy, or dogma; it is a spiritual democracy in which all can participate. The shamanic journey is certainly one of the most reliable, consistent, and accessible techniques for shifting into an altered state of consciousness to explore nonordinary reality.

The shamanic journey has deservedly become prevalent as an all-purpose facilitating method for personal practice and forms the basis for healing methods such as *soul retrieval* (which I write about in the next chapter). While journeying, the normal rules of Newtonian three-dimensional existence are demolished and travel to other worlds, precognition, and remote viewing are all possible. Put another way, the journeyer travels outside of linear, sequential time.

The human body and sensory systems have remained unchanged for millennia; our ancestors lived in, studied, and observed the same world that we occupy. So as we embark on our journey of exploration of the hidden realms, everything is eminently rediscoverable. The physical universe is perceived through the physical senses, so it stands to reason that we need to develop our nonphysical senses of awareness if we wish to perceive the nonphysical, energetic reality.

Metaphor connects supposedly unrelated elements and concepts. Metaphor traverses restricted linguistic and conceptual "no-go" areas and builds bridges across vast chasms of the unknown. In the world of multidimensional reality, the laws of metaphor and correspondence govern in place of the laws of rational thought, logic, and mental analysis.

With this in mind, we have the ability to perceive this vast unseen universe, and it is iniquitous that historically Western society has persecuted people who have navigated these realms or followed the path of extrasensory awareness. This is still within living memory, for in the United Kingdom the last prosecution under the Witchcraft Act took place in 1944. This anachronistic law was finally repealed in 1951. This opens the door to an intriguing anomaly, namely, if people in earlier times were tortured and put to death for communing with supernatural beings, how should we address religions that openly claim to represent supernatural entities? Can those be considered acceptable and become institutionalized in our society? How about testing their claims in a court of law? This is obviously a rhetorical question, but, nevertheless, it would promise to be an interesting case.

We can learn how to explore and discover these ineffable realms, and this vast unseen universe can indeed be perceived. In many years of holding workshops, I have established a working theory that there are exactly three and one-half ways of perception that people experience on their shamanic journeys.

- People in their "mind's eye" see imagery, pictures, or perhaps a visual drama or story. Sometimes the imagery can be vivid and very lucid, other times a bit misty and indistinct. Nevertheless, the main perception is through visual awareness.

- People perceive through one of the other five senses, such as hearing, smell, or taste.
- People perceive through a kinesthetic sense. This involves an intuitive knowing or a feeling in the body. They just know without any need for interpretation.
- In the third-and-a-half way, people who have the kinesthetic ability also have an extra deluxe feature in which their mind produces imagery that precisely conforms to what they are experiencing kinesthetically. The irony here is that people who perceive in this way more often than not say, "I am making this up," and they may then either dismiss or diminish their experience.

An important point is that one way is not better than another. They all can deliver an understanding of the "other" reality. Western society, however, tends to focus on visual awareness, and this emphasis appears in phrases such as "nice to see you," "I see what you mean," and "see you soon." Very few people (unless they are in an intimate relationship . . . and even then) would tend to say "nice to smell you." As a consequence, people often place a higher value on visual impressions or make imagery the sole criterion for a successful journey. Nonvisual sensory experiences are often ignored or deprecated.

The various forms of extrasensory perception are different strands of a single system, and our consciousness interprets these sensations and translates them into meaningful information. The psyche and our senses operate in conjunction as an ultrareceptive wireless receiver that gathers and decodes the bioelectric field into imagery, sound, smell, taste, and feeling, creating a metacognitive map—the *sixth sense*.

We all possess this sixth sense, or gut intuition, albeit developed to varying degrees. We experience this in our everyday lives. For example, we pick up on a highly charged electric atmosphere where there has just been an intense quarrel. Perhaps while waiting in a hospital emergency room we pick up the atmosphere of people frightened, anxious, or simply bored with waiting for hours on end, and this leads to feeling debilitated. On the other hand, when we visit a shrine, a memorial, or a place where people have been sanctified and blessed, a place that contains beautiful art, we feel uplifted and enhanced by the harmonious ambience. Spending time in nature, away from the city, also provides a boost to our feelings of well-being. A traditional remedy for poor health and recuperating after a serious illness was to convalesce by the seaside or lakeside to take advantage of the invigorating atmosphere.

I can say that some of my most profound work in the alternate reality has resulted from my auditory and olfactory senses, rather than my visual abilities. I am fortunate that I have the ability to perceive in all the above ways, and I find that each way supports the other sensing methods. The kinesthetic manner may not be glamorous, like a moving picture story, but it is quick, direct, and effective. Some of the best journeyers I know employ this characteristic in their perception.

Now we come to the big question of trust. This is the challenging matter, to trust your experience. At the beginning you don't know, there is no frame of reference for you to establish the veracity of your experience. In time, however, practice and feedback from others will help you become proficient, and gradually you learn to trust. In fact, "not knowing," or being in a place of innocence, is a good, solid position to start from. Based on years of observation and interaction with workshop participants, I have developed three fundamental keys that can make this process easier.

## THE KEYS OF TRANSFORMATION

### Intention

All actions begin with an intention, a desire for a specific outcome. Take, for instance, the process of traveling by train. You typically need to know your destination; otherwise, boarding the train would be aimless and quite purposeless. Similarly, when engaging in a shamanic ceremony or healing practice, you need to know what you want to accomplish or where you want to go. Only when this is known can your energy start to align with your intent. This is the first step. Another way of understanding this is that in the nondefinable realm of energy, your intention is a declaration: "Energy, I want you to move to that place."

## Trust

Trust takes time, and there is no shortcut or magic wand to attain this. Trust is something you feel in your gut. Gaining trust is an ongoing series of actions, feedback, and validation. "Trust but verify" is a good practice to live by, and when you share your perceptions with another person, ask for feedback that will let you know whether your perceptions are on the right track. This kind of feedback is direct and powerful. If feedback verifies your perceptions, then that is really encouraging, and it allows you to work with increasing confidence. To use a well-worn platitude, "Rome was not built in a day." There is another add-on Howard platitude, "But when it was built, it was around for a few hundred years." So don't give up. Your intention is a very powerful tool.

## Attention

Energy flows where attention goes. This principle addresses applying and focusing one's energy and intention. When you set out to do something, give it your utmost best, your maximum, your 100 percent. If you don't, the only person who gets short-changed is yourself. The principle of attention is really helpful when applied to sensing and interpreting energy. When you apply maximum focus while attuning to a person's field of energy, you can then perceive information stored within that field. By maximum attention, I do not by any means suggest that you should strain yourself and work very hard at it. In fact, I mean the opposite; the key here is to be relaxed, to still the mind and allow any thoughts floating around to dissipate, let your mind become like a tranquil lake; only then will you find that your awareness heightens and you become perceptive to a person's field of energy. Many times at workshops, I have been delighted by people's excitement, feedback, and comments when applying this principle; they say, "I can see colors around the person" and "I can see the aura."

Attention in the nondefinable realm of energy is closely linked with intent. With intention, you signal energy to move to a place, and with attention, you hold that energy at that place. Remember, it's not about straining your brain; it's about focus and a quiet state of mind.

## MAPPING THE SHAMANIC JOURNEY

The traditional shamanic map of the upper, lower, and middle worlds provides a structure that can help us understand and explore the mysteries of creation and the human consciousness. It should not be considered a literal map of "fixed" places, but rather as a guidebook for spiritual seekers. Multidimensional reality is an energetic realm, individually subjective and shaped by our cultural standpoint. In many respects, when we venture into this ancient cosmology, we move into the mysterious, magical world of metaphor rather than the systemized universe.

### The Upper World

The upper world is the traditional place of gods, ancestors, and spirit teachers. It has many names: the skyworld, the overworlds, the celestial heavens, and the kingdom of heaven. To go there, we start in a place in our imagination, a place where we can go up or ascend, such as a tree or staircase. From there, we move upward, by climbing the tree, ascending a mountain, climbing a rainbow, rising on a plume of smoke, being lifted by a whirlwind, climbing a pyramid or Ziggurat, and so on. We find echoes of this in our folklore with tales such as "Jack and the Beanstalk," in which Jack ascends a stout vine, enters an enchanted kingdom, and meets a giant; *The Wizard of Oz,* in which Dorothy is transported by tornado into a magical world; and *Alice in Wonderland,* in which Alice enters another realm through a rabbit hole, evocative of a journey to the lower world.

While the words *upper* and *lower* possess a qualitative connotation in Western culture, it's important to point out that the upper world is not better than the lower world. In the shamanic cosmological system, they complement each other, just like the roots, the trunk, and the leaves of a tree. We can also gain an appreciation of the complementary nature of the upper and lower worlds by exploring systems of spiritual belief. Shamanism and Buddhism are complementary in some respects. Shamanism gravitates toward alignment with the natural world, or instincts, and the cultivation of personal power, or life force. In Buddhist terms, these concepts align with the lower chakras. In Buddhist practice, the emphasis is on shifting the attention to the higher chakras to develop compassion and wisdom, and to encourage the loss of self (the ego self). In Tibetan and Korean Buddhism, which were both strongly influenced by their native shamanic cultures, it is important to develop one's center (the third chakra) and to integrate the natural, instinctive life force with the higher spiritual centers. Viewing these practices as a whole, it is clear that both polarities are necessary, and one is not more important than the other. It is about being in balance. The shamanic journey requires volition and discipline. The journey in itself is not the objective. The objective is to return to the everyday world and implement the knowledge that was gained during the journey.

In Western culture we separate our everyday life and the spiritual life. This creates a fragmented worldview, as opposed to the belief that in essence we are spiritual beings who happen to be in physical bodies who are having an experience in a physical universe. Viewed from this perspective, everything we do is spiritual. To illustrate this, back in the 1990s I had a "midlife existential crisis," and I quit my well-paying executive job as a manager in an American computer corporation. During that period my marriage also came to an amicable end. In retrospect, I can see that it was an inevitable time of transformation due to the upheaval in my life following my elevator accident.

Once I no longer had the company Mercedes, I bought an old British sports car, a MGB Roadster. Eventually I realized that this car was really unsuitable. It was too small, terribly uncomfortable, and cold in winter. So I decided to sell the car, but no matter how hard I tried, it just wouldn't sell.

One day, I had the bright idea to do a shamanic journey and ask a spirit teacher how I could sell the car. I journeyed to the upper world and asked the spirit teacher I met there how I could sell the car. The answer was clear and concise: "Take all of your personal possessions out of the car, and then take the car to the garage and get it repaired and working well. Then you will sell the car." I ignored this advice because I did not want to spend money on a car that I was trying to sell. About four months later the car totally broke down—it wouldn't go anywhere—so I reluctantly decided to get it repaired. The car was away for a week and cost a fair amount of money, yet when I got it back it drove fabulously; the engine roared, the steering was precise, it was great fun. The day after leaving the repair shop, I received a phone call. "Is your car still for sale?" The car was sold the next day, and then I realized that I had exactly, albeit *unwittingly,* carried out the recommendations from the spirit teacher; that is, all my stuff was out of the car, and it was working well. In fact, it was in top-notch condition, so it was gratifying that the buyer would be happy too.

## EXERCISE

### ✳ Journey to the Upper World to Meet a Teacher

You will need either a shamanic journey drumming track or a friend with a drum. Read the exercise instructions carefully before starting the journey. The suggested length for an initial journey is twenty minutes. Later, after you're comfortable with journeying, extend the length to thirty or forty minutes.

To begin, find a place where you feel comfortable and will not be disturbed for about an hour. When you are ready, either lie down or sit in a comfortable chair and darken the room, or at least cover your eyes. (It is easier to carry out this type of visionary work in subdued light.) Remove or release any tight or restrictive clothing, and shift your breathing to a gentle rhythm. As you breathe, allow yourself to become rooted by feeling a magnetic pull into the ground.

Now is the time to focus on the first key of transformation, intention. In your mind, focus on your intention; contemplate the purpose of the journey and what you want to achieve. Through this process, you align your energy with your thoughts and the hoped-for outcome. For the purposes of this journey, the intention is to journey to the upper world to meet a spirit teacher. Additionally (or on a subsequent journey), you may want to ask a question. If this is the case, I advise that you make it an important question, maybe one of the most important questions in your life. It doesn't have to be a "spiritual" question; remember, your whole life is a spiritual experience.

When you are ready, in your imagination allow yourself to be in a place you know that reminds you of Earth. When I say a place you know, I mean a place that you have visited or have seen in a film or photograph. In any case, make it a real place. This place also needs something that allows you to go up, such as a tree, a hill, or a pyramid. Take the time you need to allow your attention to inhabit this place. Have a sense of being there: feel your feet on the ground; sense the earth pushing up against your soles and between your toes; feel the wind around you, perhaps blowing through the trees or carrying the scent of wildflowers. Just relax into the feeling of being present there.

Now, look at the location where you intend to go up and start making your ascent. During this ascent be aware of passing through a "layer" of some sort. This layer could be experienced as something ephemeral, such as clouds or even tissue paper. Some people sense it kinesthetically. You could also feel like you are moving through a membrane. This is the separator between the realms. Once you have moved through this layer, you will be in the upper world.

People experience the appearance of the upper world in various ways. Our psyche interprets the intangible attributes of nonordinary reality in a manner that we can understand. It is a subjective, not a generic, interpretation, although cultural background extends a major influence. Nevertheless, in general people describe the upper world as having an ethereal quality, illuminated with soft colors.

Now it is time to explore. Go ahead and walk around, remembering your intention. Perceive this place using every sensory system that you possess. During this journey you may come across beings in human form. When you meet one of these beings, ask him or her, "Are you my spirit teacher?" You may get one of the following three responses.

**Yes.** If the response is yes, then relax and engage with this experience. How are you feeling? How does he or she appear to you? Don't be shy; greet the spirit teacher, feel free to speak, and ask a question if you have one. If you don't have a specific question, ask the spirit teacher how he or she will be helping and guiding you. Ask about any influences the teacher could bring into your life.

**No.** If the response is no, then continue to explore until the above occurs.

**No,** and the spirit points in a particular direction. If this takes place, then go in the indicated direction. If the being points upward, that's okay. Just go and find a place in the upper world where you can again make an ascent. There are many levels in the upper world, and as you ascend be aware of the separators between these levels. At the next level again explore until you meet your spirit teacher.

### ✛ Coming Back

Coming back is all important, and it needs to be integrated into your intention, either spoken or unspoken. This work has no point unless you come back into the physical world to build your bridge between the manifest and the unmanifest realities.

Returning can take place either at a prearranged time with your drumming friend or when you hear the call-back drumming rhythm on your shamanic journeying track. Coming back requires volition and discipline, particularly because sometimes you might be journeying in a place from which you do not want to return. When you hear the call-back signal, stop what you are doing, say your farewells, turn around, and return the same way that you came. Make your descent, and when you have arrived in the place that you started from, the place in your imagination that reminded you of Earth, become aware of that place, feel your feet on the ground and the grass or soil pushing up against the soles of your feet. Be back in the physical world.

Then either relate your journey to your companion or make a note in your journal. This is a helpful practice because sometimes when you write or tell of your experience, seemingly unrelated events during the journey click into place.

One of the things I enjoy most during workshops is when participants tell me that "nothing" happened on their journey. I then ask them to tell me precisely what "nothing" took place. Time after time I have been amazed when some of the most wonderful, poetic, and powerful experiences are expressed. Remember, the rational mind is not an ally in this work. Don't judge or evaluate the experience; often the circumstances of the journey, the landscape, and the environment have much to say. Be neutral and just say or write what happened; the personal revelation may happen a little later. Things may take time to percolate.

Sometimes during early journeys, a moment before the call back sounds, the spirit teacher may start to tell the person something really important, maybe of seemingly "cosmic" significance. Even though the spirit is about to reveal the secrets of the universe, it is time to come back! It is the spirit teacher's way of telling you to come back again, in a similar fashion to a television cliff-hanger. The spirits also have a sense of humor. Remember your intention, and engage your volition and discipline to return.

### The Lower World

The lower world is often experienced as a place of nurturing and sustenance. There is also a link between the lower world and the physical world.

People often experience a feeling of union with Earth in their journeys, but some may experience discomfort and turbulence in the lower world, which may be a reflection of their inner landscape. Some also experience fear of the "descent," or of going down, a fear I believe to be substantially induced by the cultural demonization of the lower world.

In the lower world you can meet spirit guides and allies, widely known as power animals, or spirit animals. For me, journeying to the lower world has been a challenging, emotionally moving, and ultimately rewarding experience. It has provided me with an important link lacking in my life, a connection with animals. On one journey, I asked a spirit animal the difference between humans and animals. The reply was, "Animals do not judge themselves!"

## Power vs. Personal Power

The word *power* is often associated with this kind of work. We use terms such as *power animal* and *gaining personal power*. But what are we talking about? What is the meaning of power? Words can be loaded with emotional meaning, and no matter how careful we are in the words we choose, they are still understood subjectively by the individual and influenced by social circumstances, life experience, early upbringing, and culture.

The word *power* in the West has perhaps an unfavorable interpretation. People often associate power with "power over something or someone else." The whole arena of "power relationships," in which we find an imbalance of power among the people involved, is undergoing a significant level of public debate in the West. This debate focuses quite rightly on the undesirable aspects, the "abuse of power"—in the community, the workplace, religious institutions, schools, police forces, and the government.

In shamanism power means only one thing, and this is power over yourself. This is personal power, which allows you to live a life of freedom, to respond rather than react, and to be centered in yourself, not blown off course by the trials and tribulations of human life. Much of the teachings of indigenous peoples converge on this principle, the gathering or stalking of power. Basically, the more power (or energy) you have, the more you can do.

The English language is lacking vocabulary and concepts in this area; we miss the subtlety of nuance. In shamanism, power corresponds with energy, or life force. This pathway also provides the opportunity to align with and draw in the universal field of energy.

## Power Animals

There are a couple of ways to view the notion of power animals. They can be seen as incorporeal allies whose role is to inform, to protect, and to bring a specific quality into alignment with ourselves. This is often a quality that we need rather than one that we desire. When exploring the invisible realms, it really helps to have a guide in the same way that if you were to take an exploration trip to another country, it would make an enormous difference if you were accompanied by a guide who knew the lay of the land and could speak the local language.

With this in mind, I encourage you to build a relationship with your animal spirit guide, a relationship that could really help to open a loving doorway of understanding and appreciation of the natural world around you, as well as help to develop and grow your own qualities.

Honor your power animal by keeping pictures around your house that remind you of it and by donating money to charities that support your particular animal or that protect endangered species. Act now to protect the animals! Don't think that one individual cannot make a difference. Human history, for better or worse, teaches us otherwise.

The other perspective is to regard power animals as a manifestation of your psyche's interpretation of the infinite multidimensional field of universal consciousness. In this case your psyche has interpreted an aspect of the universal mind as a powerful symbol that embodies the qualities relevant and meaningful to you.

It doesn't matter which view you hold. The only thing that matters is whether it works. I personally feel comfortable with the ambiguity of holding both perspectives.

<u>EXERCISE</u>

## ✳ Journey to the Lower World to Meet a Power Animal

You will need either a shamanic journey drumming track or a friend with a drum. Read the exercise instructions carefully before starting the journey. The suggested length for an initial journey is twenty minutes. Later, after you're comfortable with journeying, extend the length to thirty or forty minutes.

To begin, find a place that you feel comfortable and will not be disturbed for about an hour. When you are ready, either lie down or sit in a comfortable chair and darken the room, or at least cover your eyes. (It is easier to carry out this type of visionary work in subdued light.) Remove or release any tight or restrictive clothing, and allow your breathing to move to a gentle rhythm. As you breathe allow yourself to feel rooted or imagine a magnetic pull into the ground.

Focus on the first key of transformation, intention. Contemplate the purpose of the journey and what you want to achieve. This process allows you to align your energy with your thoughts and hoped-for outcome. For the purposes of this journey, the intention is to journey to the lower world to meet a power animal. Additionally (or for a subsequent journey), you may want to ask a question. If this is the case, I advise that you make it an important question, maybe one of the most important questions in your life.

When you are ready, in your imagination allow yourself to be in a place you know that reminds you of Earth. It could be a place you have visited or have seen in a film or photograph. In any event, make it a real place. It requires an entry point that allows you to go down. Well-trod examples of this are a cave entrance, a hole in the ground, an animal burrow, a body of water, a well shaft, and as a modern urban example, a subway entrance.

Take the time you need to allow your attention to be in this place. Have a sense of being there: feel your feet on the ground; sense the earth pushing up against your soles and between your toes; feel the wind around you, perhaps blowing through the trees. Just relax into the feeling of being there.

Before you move into the entrance to the lower world, focus on your intention, in this case to journey to the lower world to meet a spirit guide in animal form. Repeat the intention; it even helps to speak this intention out loud. When you are ready, move into the entrance, which typically will lead into a tunnel that can be in either earth or water. This tunnel may be experienced as a spiral, straight and smooth, or straight with a ribbed motif. Some people walk down the tunnel, some run, some free fall, some slide down. There is no right way or wrong way to go down; just continue to descend until you arrive at your destination.

The lower world may appear in one of two ways. You may arrive in an area that resembles the landscape of this world, such as by a river, a sea, mountains, forests, or meadows, or you may arrive in what I call the "bus stop," or terminus. This is often experienced as a cave or a cavernlike place. If you come into this place, that is okay; you will find it very easy to find an exit into the landscape of the lower world. There will be an opening of some sort: a door, a window, or just an open space. Make your way through this opening and into the open landscape.

Use all your sensory systems to take stock of your surroundings, and remember that your power animal will be attempting to attract your attention. Make a note of where you are, and keep track of your movements in the lower world. You may be aware of the presence of animals. Does one stand out in some way? If so, move toward the animal if it hasn't yet moved toward you. How do you feel about the animal? Do not be concerned if it has a ferocious manner. That is fine.

Examine your feelings about the animal you encounter. If you are not sure or are feeling circumspect about it, start to move away. If it is your power animal, it will make an effort to reveal itself to you, and it may show itself on multiple occasions in various guises. After it shows itself to you three or four times, simply ask, "Are you my power animal?" Pay attention to the response. The animal may visibly demonstrate to you in "mime" style that the answer is either yes or no. Another way of receiving an answer is through telepathy, or hearing the answer as spoken words in your head. If the animal turns around and moves away, don't see this as a nonaffirmative response. It may want you to follow in order to show you something or to take you to a specific place.

If the answer is no, then continue your search until you encounter another animal, and repeat the procedure. If the response is yes, then spend some time with the power animal. Ask it about the qualities it brings for you. Again, pay great attention to what happens next. If you do not understand the answer, ask again or request that the animal show you in a different way.

When you have understood and are satisfied with the answer or as soon as it is time to return (this can be determined either by setting a prearranged time with your drumming friend or by using the call-back rhythm on your shamanic journeying track), say your farewells and retrace your path to your entry point into the lower world. Once you are there, move into the entrance and begin your ascent. You will find it very easy to return. You may experience a wind or a sense of pressure forcing you upward until you return to the place where you started from, the place that reminded you of Earth, the place that you know.

Then either relate your journey to your companion or make a note in your journal. This is a helpful practice because sometimes when you write or tell of your experience, seemingly unrelated events and details click into place.

It is worth noting that various books and publications supply lists of animals and the qualities inherent in each species. However, to develop a close relationship with the power animal, you must get to know it personally. While the traits of the species might come into play, there will often be very specific qualities about your individual power animal that are linked especially to you. You may find that the spirit animal knows you well, including your personal history, your strengths, and your weaknesses. Remember, these may well be qualities you *need* rather than qualities you *want,* and in that you have to be brutally honest with yourself.

### + Suggestions for Further Journeys

Once you have met and engaged with your power animal, on subsequent journeys you can ask questions or ask for insights into your life. I would suggest that you avoid questions that begin with the phrase "should I?" If you are candid you likely know the answer to that; it's just that for whatever reason you are reluctant to accept it. Also, the way in which a question is posed often influences the answer. For example, "Should I live in Manchester?" would elicit different answers than "What would be the benefits if I were to live in Manchester?" with the latter perhaps being more comprehensive and useful.

## The Middle World

The middle world refers to the physical world we inhabit, an unseen, nonordinary reality version of the physical world. It is considered a place where illnesses and diseases first manifest, like an energetic intrusion moving into the physical body. The spirits of deceased people also inhabit the middle world. They may be unaware that they are dead or have too much of an attachment to the physical plane. This is an important area that I'll be covering later in further detail.

The middle world is the energetic realm directly influenced by human beings, and entering this dimension can present challenges. Just consider our history of violence, destruction, atrocities, and warfare. The places where these events occurred can continue to hold a detrimental vibrational field for many years. This was clearly demonstrated to me a few years prior to my accident when I visited the Dachau Nazi concentration camp. As soon as I got out of my vehicle just outside the camp gates, my knees turned to jelly, my legs gave way, and I fell down onto the ground. Later, while walking through the camp buildings and into the gas chamber, I again collapsed, pushed to the floor by the weight of an oppression and terror so heavy it was indescribable. I had to crawl on my hands and knees to escape. I didn't understand what was happening at the time, but now I certainly would not enter into such a situation without serious preparation and a focused awareness.

Some years ago I was asked to help people who lived in a house in the country where all sorts of unpleasant incidents were happening. This was a small community house, and they were experiencing constant nightmares, feeling uncomfortable, being argumentative whenever they were in the house together, and even at times feeling suicidal. As I arrived at the house, I felt a sense of foreboding and heightened fear. I took a walk around the residential grounds with an increasing state of attention. A few hundred yards from the house, these feelings intensified, and in my mind's eye I could see people being pursued and killed by medieval soldiers. I felt the terror and anguish of these people as I watched this appalling slaughter. My attention was drawn to a narrow gully where bodies were being dumped. I observed streams of blood flowing down this gully, and I followed the gully downhill. It led directly to the back door of the house (which was on level ground). This is where the flow of blood accumulated, linking the house to the location of this massacre.

I met with the community members and after deliberation we carried out a memorial ceremony at the massacre site on behalf of the people who had been slain. We placed gifts in the gully where the bodies had been dumped, dedicating these to the spirits of the place. We all experienced a feeling of relief and peace after this. I advised them to dig up the gully adjacent to the house, replace the soil, and "sweeten" the ground by planting an herb garden. I later heard from them that the nightmares had ceased, the feelings of fear had lifted, and the atmosphere had considerably improved.

I need to emphasize that the middle world is not a bad place; it expresses the dichotomy present in the physical world—the good, the bad, and the in between, gray areas. Many parts of the world have been loved, cherished, and blessed by people for generations. I was reminded of this when I was considering buying my house in London; the rear garden was bordered by an old Victorian cemetery. I thought that cemeteries are "spooky" places, so I decided to go in there and walk around. As I entered the grounds and moved into an expanded state of attention, I became aware of the force of the many beautiful old chestnut and oak trees, and I realized that the place had experienced a great deal of love and beauty in the good thoughts and sincere prayers that people had made for their deceased loved ones. The place resonated with beauty. That experience was an outstanding teaching for me and certainly cleared my preconceptions about cemeteries.

Additional middle world activities include the CIA remote viewing program during the Cold War and the equivalent KGB psychic warfare division. These agencies utilized intricate and detailed procedures and, of course, the objective was to carry out espionage and disrupt the opposing side. The millions of dollars and rubles invested in these programs illustrate the importance and value of this work to these governmental agencies, which very much regarded themselves as operating in the real world.

I personally tend to be circumspect about middle world journeys, precisely for the reason that I have outlined, which is that there is a lot of unpleasant energetic debris out there that we humans have created. I suggest as a precaution that you undertake middle world journeys only when you have developed some experience or established a relationship with your spirit teachers and power animals, as they will offer you guidance.

Now we come to the question of intention. What is your intention in the middle world? I suggest that if you are searching for guidance, advice, and teaching, then go to either the upper world or the lower world. However, if you are looking for the whereabouts of an object that you have lost or want to find out where someone is, then a middle world journey could be appropriate. Another reason to journey in the middle world is to assist deceased human beings in making their transition to the places people go when they die, rather than lingering in a state of confusion or even unaware that they have passed away. This work, although distressing at times, is powerful and beautiful. Those who engage in it are known by the Greek term *psychopomp,* meaning "conductor of souls." This body of work is covered in a later chapter.

## EXERCISE

### ✳ Exploration Journey to the Middle World

For this exercise I propose two simple explorations. The first journey is to a familiar place that has pleasant memories and connotations for you. The second is to a place you haven't physically been to yet but would like to visit. For the latter you will need an image from a photograph or a film. Follow the same procedure for both journeys with the exception of a modified intention.

You will need either a shamanic journey drumming track or a friend with a drum. Read the exercise instructions carefully before starting the journey. The suggested length for an initial journey is ten minutes. Later, after you are comfortable with journeying, extend the length to twenty or thirty minutes.

To begin, find a place where you feel comfortable and will not be disturbed for about an hour. When you are ready, either lie down or sit in a comfortable chair and darken the room, or at least cover your eyes. (It is easier to carry out this type of visionary work in subdued light.) Remove or release any tight or restrictive clothing, and allow your breathing to move to a gentle rhythm. As you breathe allow yourself to feel rooted or perhaps feel a kind of magnetic pull to the ground. Now is the time to focus on the first key of transformation, intention.

Contemplate the purpose of the journey and what you want to achieve. This process allows you to align your energy with your thoughts and hoped-for outcome. For the purposes of this journey, the intention is to journey to the middle world to visit and explore a place that you know. For the second journey, the intention is to journey to the location that you have decided to visit and explore the area.

When you are ready, in your imagination allow yourself to travel to a place that you know. Relax and take the time that you need to allow your attention to inhabit this place. Have a sense of being there: feel your feet on the ground; sense the earth pushing up against the soles of your feet; feel the wind around you; listen to the breeze blowing through the trees.

When you have a sense of your surroundings, walk around and extend your perceptions. Feel the ground underneath your feet. Is it soft, spongy, or firm? Sense the air and wind around you. What does it feel like to breathe in this place? Can you hear anything? Listen carefully. Can you smell anything, such as grass or flowers? What scents or odors are carried with the breeze? Use every sensory system in this exploration. Does the place appear different; are the colors the same; are trees around? If so, greet the trees.

Does anything happen? Do you perceive a response? Spend time in this place until the call-back drumming sounds.

Then either relate your journey to your companion or make a note in your journal. This is a helpful practice because sometimes when you write or tell of your experience, seemingly unrelated events during the journey click into place.

Your consciousness and imaginative abilities hold great power; exercise them as often as you can. Painting, craftwork, reading, making music—any creative endeavor will expand your abilities, which you can harness to empower your life through the practices above.

# 5

# SOUL RETRIEVAL

*The soul is not in the body, but the body in the soul.*

ALAN WATTS

For thousands of years the most prodigious philosophers, sages, and theologians have attempted to define the soul. A copious number of treatises and books endeavor to nail down this concept. More than two thousand years ago, Greek philosopher and scientist Aristotle, in his book *De Anima* (*On the Soul*), acknowledged that this is one of the most challenging enigmas for a philosopher to master. In Greek, the word for soul is *psyche,* and this term in contemporary usage has varying interpretations. It is worth noting that the term *psychology* literally means "study of the soul," and euphoniously speaking it rolls off the tongue more easily than, say, "soulology."

Several definitions for the soul are in existence today, so to provide a working definition in a healing and transformative context is difficult but necessary; I refer to the soul as *life force*. This is the life force that animates our physical life on Earth. Our soul is metaphorically in the body, in our guts. It responds to life, to rhythm, to joy, to music. Otis Redding singing "Sittin' on the Dock of the Bay," Paul Robeson singing

"Ol' Man River"—that's soul to me. What moves our soul also moves our body. The African saying "If I can talk, I can sing. If I can walk, I can dance" speaks about soul. The purpose of soul retrieval is to gather as much of our life force as possible in order to live this life to the greatest degree that we can as human beings. In many respects, there is nothing "sacred" or extraordinary about this per se; it is a natural expression of life.

Circumventing the definition debate, my subjective perspective and vision of the soul, or life force, is of a biogeometric structure that contains our memories, our emotions, and our experiences from our very beginning in the physical world, the moment of our conception. I usually describe the soul using the metaphor of a three-dimensional tapestry with a geometric structure consisting of threads, fibers, and filaments. Each thread is a discrete element, a story or an experience that stretches back in time. In addition, these threads form part of a larger geometric structure that includes our parents and our personal ancestry, which also stretches back in time and is part of a larger, more encompassing structure, and so on. If you follow this to the ultimate conclusion, we are an integral part of an all-encompassing biogeometric structure, and I refer to this as planet Earth and, by extension, the universe.

When people say to me "I want to heal the Earth" or "The Earth needs healing," I suggest to them that the key to this is in healing themselves. If we are an intrinsic part of the Earth, then personal healing and transformation are explicitly influencing the *anima mundi,* the soul of the world. This is nothing new or fanciful. The understanding that humanity is a strand in the "web of life" is part of an inspirational ecological philosophy of the Native Americans. As a pithy Lakota proverb puts it, "The frog does not drink up the pond in which he lives."

Soul retrieval is one of the most effective and well-known practices to restore lost life force. The loss of life force is known as *soul loss,* and this can take place when we suffer a trauma, have an accident, separate from a partner, experience the death of a loved one, or go through a pervasive period of difficult circumstances. When we undergo a severe trauma, typically a part of our life force goes away so that we can survive whatever is happening to us. It is a way for the body and consciousness to survive the trauma. Problems develop when the soul part or fragment does not return.

Often soul loss happens when we are very young and are without a frame of reference for the experience, and we are therefore unaware of the dissonance within our being and the unconscious disruptive patterns that repeat in our lives because of that early soul loss. In some way we are endeavoring to reclaim our lost life force by repeating and reexperiencing the emotional wound over and over again. This can be very painful to live through, but we need to know that our consciousness, in a consummate self-revealing function, is showing us that we need to restore our life force and heal.

Shamanism does not dwell on past events; there is only a vast, awesome, ever-moving, great moment of now in which there is no separate past, present, or future. A practitioner can journey outside of linear time to go to the place where that traumatic event is still occurring for a person, locate that person's life force, which is held in that energetic event, and restore it. When this has been carried out, the deep healing can truly begin.

The concept of soul loss and the ceremonial retrieval of souls are found in many cultures. For example, in the Tibetan Bon tradition, one of the most important practices performed by Tibetan shamans of the Sichen path is soul retrieval, of which there are two forms—*lalu,* meaning redeeming, or buying back the soul (the vital energy or core essence), and *chilu,* redeeming the life energy (the energy that maintains the functions of the mind and body). These practices are separate rites in the Bon tradition and are widespread not only in the Bon tradition but in all Tibetan Buddhist schools.[1]

Across the globe, the great visionary artist and sage Pablo Amaringo, from the Amazon rainforest, created a painting based on traditional Amazonian lore entitled *Searching for the Lost Soul,* in which he describes the shaman recovering a lost soul that has been taken by a sorcerer and restoring it to the body.

In the Peruvian Andes, musicologist and author Peter Cloudsley and I asked local traditional curandera Doris Rivera Lenz whether the concept of soul loss is known in the Andean culture. She replied, "Yes, when a child has an accident or suffers a traumatic event, its soul can leave its body and it may get ill. This is known as *susto*. If this happens, an offering is made in the place of the accident to heal the child" (see color plate 2). She continued, "There are many ways to call the soul. You can get hold of a piece of the person's clothing, make a little doll, and decorate it with flowers or something that the person finds attractive, and you call the soul in the place where the fright took place. You can call up elements like herbs, a dove's nest, feathers, tobacco, or coca leaves. However, before you begin the ceremony, you must first ask permission from Pachamama (Mother Earth)."

A number of symptoms are associated with soul loss; for example, people feeling that they are observing life as an outsider, rather than engaging and being fully involved; feeling that they are "spaced out" a lot of the time, not really present in life; experiencing pervasive fear, or an inability to trust people. I have also found that severe depression can be a symptom of soul loss. Chronic illness may also be a symptom, and this directly relates to personal power or life force. In the shamanic worldview, power and health go hand in hand. If the body is "powerfull," there is no room for illness or disease, which are often regarded as invasive forces.

In my practice I have worked with many people who have undertaken considerable work on an original trauma but who remained stuck in their recovery. The concept of soul loss as a survival mechanism is understood and termed *dissociation* in modern psychology. The fundamental difference between soul retrieval and psychotherapy is that soul retrieval focuses on the return and integration of the lost life force, rather than on the original trauma itself. Psychotherapy does not ask, "Where is the lost soul part, and how do we get it back?" In my experience soul retrieval and therapy combine well together. The most beneficial approach is first the recapitulation of the lost life force, followed by therapy to support the person through the process of consciously integrating the uncomfortable feelings as they unravel and are released. The unraveling of the emotional filaments can be a challenging process because the person may experience the raw pain of the original emotions. This is a fundamental part of the transitory healing process. There is no shortcut; when deep wounds heal, painful feelings are released. However, this phase will pass. In Amazonian terms, this is called *purging*. It is a form of liberation that allows a person to move forward and live a life of fulfillment.

Earlier I advanced the notion that the threads contained in our individual soul connect to larger structures, or fields, of consciousness. Here is a story (out of many) that illustrates this; the name has been changed for privacy. Helga, a German woman in her early thirties, came to see me with severe asthma, which she had suffered most of her life. I must point out that her intention was purely to relieve the asthma and not to pursue any soul retrieval or related work.

As I made my initial energetic connection to her, I felt an overpowering sense of smothering, oppression, and choking. The feeling was so strong that it didn't seem possible that it came from her. I started to energetically move through the layers of her soul tapestry, and as I followed a thread I entered Germany during the Nazi era. I saw swastikas and heard voices and the marching music of that time. Although it was all unexpected, I have learned through experience to trust my vision and intuition; after all, I was following the thread of her asthma.

I suggested that I take a shamanic journey to explore the source of her asthma. She agreed, and I started to journey. At my initial "conference" with the spirit guides, they issued me with a gas mask. Again, this was unexpected, but I put it on and moved through the entrance. I came into a town filled with thick yellowish pungent fumes. I walked around the town covered in this thick yellowish fog, and then I felt a "pull," a kind of magnetic attraction to enter a particular house. I went in and descended to the cellar, where I found Helga as a young girl of about eight or nine. She was sitting against a wall with her knees drawn to her chest in great fear and anxiety. I gently approached her, told her who I was, and explained that I was there to rescue her and take her home to her future projection. I speak German well enough to have said soothing words in her mother language. She responded warmly and was very willing to return with me and leave her dismal hiding place.

I brought her back. In that reality she was a little girl, and in our physical reality that little girl represented energy, or life force. I blew the returned soul part into Helga's chest, at which she let out an enormous shudder. Very deep breathing followed this release. Helga immediately stated that she felt energized, clearer, and lighter in her body, and she didn't have the feeling of being crushed in her chest.

Once she had rested, we spoke again, and she told me that in the town where she had been born and had spent her early years there was a factory where the poisonous Zyklon B gas used in the Nazi extermination camps was manufactured. She said, "Although everybody knew this, no one ever talked about it or mentioned it." This young woman who had not even been born at the time of World War II had suffered what I can only describe as an existential trauma. Her lifelong breathing predicament connects directly to the poisoned atmosphere (*figuratively* speaking) of this town and its dark secret.

A few weeks after our session, Helga called me and said that the asthma had vanished, she could breathe well again, and she felt as if a great weight had been lifted from her. She was very happy, and she said that the night after her soul retrieval she had gone to bed early and had had the best night's sleep for ages. The following days she had felt joyful, yet with a tinge of sadness as some of the emotions relating to the retrieval worked through her. It took about two weeks until she really felt good about herself. She was delighted to have this confirmed by the people around her, who said that she looked radiant. I too was delighted to hear this.

This acted as a reminder to me that concealing dark secrets creates a soul wound, whether in the individual or the collective. The clear implication is that atrocious and heinous events in the history of a people or a nation need to be brought out into the light of day. The truth, however painful, can lead to healing and reconciliation. This concept is valid on both the personal and collective level.

After a serious accident or major surgery, I hear people say, "I haven't felt the same since then." Dr. Steven Cartwright, a homeopathic doctor who was awarded the prestigious Churchill Scholarship to conduct a field trip to Peru for studying indigenous medicines, wrote following a soul retrieval session with me. During the field visit he had suffered serious injuries in a road accident.

> I had been involved in a road accident five months previously that had left me with a badly broken leg, and I was in an awful state of depression, lacking energy and vitality. I could only describe it as feeling that I was "not here." I felt half dead to the world, really unable to function effectively or with any enthusiasm.
>
> During the soul retrieval session, it was explained to me that a large part of my life force had left at the time of the accident and was still at the scene in a state of shock. The road scene described matched the actual place. I realized that it was true, and that I wasn't here—I was five thousand miles away in Peru!
>
> Within minutes of the soul retrieval, when my lost soul parts were being blown back into me, I felt alive again for the first time in five months. The effect was so dramatic—enthusiasm, vitality, energy, and joy returned. It was like something that I had never experienced before.
>
> It's been some weeks now since the soul retrieval, and I can say it's been the most extraordinary therapeutic experience I have ever had. I feel that I am "here" again, back home.

One of the essential characteristics of life force is that it contains memories, and in piecemeal fashion following a soul retrieval, memories join together similar to a jigsaw puzzle, piece by piece. The psyche does this as a way to shield the person from being overwhelmed at the sudden return of distressing memories. Never has this been more remarkably demonstrated to me than when working with a woman whose returning memories led to the police reopening a forty-one-year-old murder case. I wrote a brief account of this story in the book *Plant Spirit Shamanism*, published in 2006. It feels appropriate to narrate the complete version in this book. I am grateful to Joanne, who gave her permission and supplied the newspaper cuttings from the 1950s.

Following a soul retrieval session, Joanne called me in consternation because certain memories were resurfacing and were causing her great discomfort. We arranged a session to address this, at which she told me that she had started to have flashbacks to when she was five years old. She was haunted by the memory that her mother had murdered a woman in the town where she grew up. She told me that the brutal stabbing of this elderly widow had shocked and traumatized the townspeople, and there was great a fear of "a murderer within our community." The police interviewed more than one thousand people in the investigation, but the murderer was never found, and the case remained unsolved for forty-one years.

Usually I am reluctant to discover things of this nature; I do not feel that it is appropriate to be involved in work where a finger could be pointed at people for their misdeeds. It could lead to becoming entangled, so I tend to be circumspect in these matters. However, this situation was different because it had risen subsequent to a soul retrieval session with me, and I was obliged to follow it through because of the responsibility I felt toward Joanne.

I journeyed back in time to the north England town of Bradford, and I alighted in one of the old-time streets. I studied the area carefully, saw the shop, and went in. Inside, I was struck by the very specific smell of old-fashioned wood lacquer accompanied by lavender and spices. I witnessed the murder inside the store, and to my astonishment I saw that the murderer was a woman disguised as a man. I followed her into the street and saw the young Joanne, whose hand was being held by her grandmother. Her grandmother had the manner and appearance of being a "lookout."

All this time I was carrying out a simultaneous narration of the journey so that Joanne could follow what I was experiencing. When the journey was completed, Joanne was in a state of sadness and relief. She told me that she knew my journey was true when I described the very distinctive smell of the wood lacquer, lavender, and spices. She knew without a shred of doubt that this event had happened and that her mother had carried out this terrible action.

A few days later Joanne called to say that more memories of that time had resurfaced. She remembered the motive for the murder: the shopkeeper was a moneylender, and her mother was in serious debt to her. She also told me that she had gone to the police, who had reopened this case; however, her mother was terminally ill, and therefore the case could not be effectively pursued.

Later, she contacted me, and I was touched by what she told me. She had gone to see her mother, who was on her deathbed. Her mother was unable to speak, but could hear. Joanne said, "Mum, I know you did it. I know you murdered her." Her mother could not speak, yet she started to cry. It was no longer a secret; this was a true confession, which at the very last moment reconciled Joanne with her mother. Shortly after this Joanne's mother went into a coma and died.

This whole story moved me, and the beauty of it was that Joanne could at last put this disturbing episode to rest and move on with her life. I was also touched that her mother could finally unburden herself of this monstrous act at the moment before she died. This doesn't take away my feelings about the clear conspiracy to murder the elderly shopkeeper, but I was very happy for Joanne.

A concluding note on this: Joanne later sent me some newspaper clippings about this murder. When I looked at the photographs, the images matched the surroundings I had seen in my journey.

## SOUL ENTANGLEMENT

Soul retrieval is one way to restore and maintain our life force and power. Through this technique we receive our own life force. Another way to maintain our life force is not to hold on to anybody else. In our lives, we take and sometimes hold on to the energy of others. Although this is often called *soul theft*, I find the term to be far too emotive and prejudicial; I prefer to call this *soul entanglement*. This is something that many of us do, and it should be looked at in a nonjudgmental way. In some respects, it is the other side of soul retrieval.

Soul entanglement can be a learned generational behavior and often occurs within families. It is an unconscious act. In fact, if the people involved knew what they were doing, they might well be very upset.

We become entangled with people's life force in many ways, as these examples illustrate:

- When we are jealous of another person's position, abilities, or status. Envy is a common cause.
- When a person wants another person's identity or feels the need to be like him or her. This also occurs when we hero worship or idolize someone.
- A very common way to take another person's power is to judge that person. An additional facet here is that the judgment on another person reveals more about the person who is making the judgment than the person being judged.
- When we overcare for someone, causing that person to become too dependent on us. This can result in the person losing the strength and will to support him- or herself.

Soul entanglement creates a number of problems:

- The life-force energy of all parties can become diminished. The entanglement becomes a burden, a weight. Interactions are sticky and inconclusive.
- Relationships can be held on to, causing difficult, ragged, and unsatisfactory completions.
- We may even take on someone else's *shadow,* and find ourselves working with another's feelings, which may be an uncomfortable and challenging experience. The "shadow" in this context refers to the Jungian metaphorical concept of our unknown, even unenlightened emotions that conflict with our conscious self or personality. These emotions are denied the light of expression within our conscious personality and hence are experienced as darker or as shadows.

Workshop participants taking part in the soul-release exercise have expressed the sensations of entanglement in a number of ways. One said that the soul parts felt like "barnacles on the hull of a ship holding me back and weighing me down." Another said, "It felt like I was covered in clinging seeds and leaves."

All parties experience benefits when we return another person's life force. This is some of the most profound and healing work individuals can undertake. I get a lot of feedback from people who do this work, and I have been told many times about relationships between partners, parents, and children changing and improving. To provide a simple analogy, it is like an energetic tug-of-war in which both parties are pulling on the rope. When one person releases the other's entangled life force, that person has effectively let go of the rope. Then when the other person responds, there is no more rope to pull or exert pressure on.

Workshop participants and clients often tell me that as soon as they did this work, they went home and cleared all the clutter and junk from their home. To me, this demonstrates a physical manifestation of the work that was done energetically. It also grounds and solidifies the intent—the desire to release. They are effectively opening creative life space and making themselves available for new things to come into their lives. This is precisely what happens in our own soul bodies: we make more space for our own life force, more space for our own power to manifest in the world.

Even though we may understand this instinctively and would like to untangle and release another person's life force, it may be difficult to recall or remember people's names or faces. Either we were embroiled in an unpleasant event or, in most cases, the act was carried out unconsciously, without awareness. This is the clear problem.

The tools, methods, and practices of shamanism can be very useful in this act of releasing. Unconscious memories are hard to access, while spirit guides and higher order consciousness* provide a means to gain entry. Spirit guides and our higher order consciousness know us perfectly: they know our personal history, our strengths, our qualities, our foibles, and our personal symbology.

## EXERCISE

## ✳ A Ceremony to Release the Life Force of Those with Whom You Are Entangled

Embark on this shamanic journey with the intention of asking the spirits to tell the names, or show the faces, or let you know in any way you can understand the people whose life force you are entangled with and are still holding on to. This journey can be carried out in either the upper or lower world. You can also meditate with this intention and allow the insights to surface.

Allow yourself about twenty minutes for this journey. You may be guided by your spirit ally to a place where people whose soul parts you are entangled with are gathered, or you may simply become aware of who they are. All methods are valid; there is no right or wrong way to do this. Sometimes

---

*Higher order consciousness* is the term I use to denote the universal interconnectivity of a vast infinite field of consciousness. We are an integral element within this field even though we may not perceive the wider field, in much the same way that an individual water droplet forms part of a raincloud.

people in the journey are guided to a lake and find reflected in the water the faces of those with whom they are entangled.

When you have returned from the journey, it is a good idea to write down the names while the memories of the journey are still fresh in your mind. Please keep in your mind that you should not judge yourself for the entanglements; it is something we all do. The difference is that you have an opportunity to restore the balance.

Now you know what you need to release and return. This can be best achieved by a ritual or ceremony. These methods have great power in this reality; they are ways of combining the heart, mind, spirit, and body in a single physical action and intention. Religions from all over the world have long recognized the importance of ritual and ceremony. They offer a means for us to communicate with spirit allies and higher order consciousness. In Western culture, we have forgotten that ordinary and nonordinary reality belong together; they are two halves of one whole.

A fire ceremony is one option for releasing soul parts. This can be carried out alone or with others, and it can be very healing if this ritual is witnessed by friends. The participants can support you by using a rattle, gently drumming, or chanting. To start the ceremony, you need a location, preferably outdoors, that provides a way to safely contain a fire. If you are holding this ceremony indoors, you will need a metal or ceramic bowl and a candle. Feel free to improvise; a wok works well too.

Call in the spirits, ask for their assistance, and state your intention very clearly: "I am releasing the soul parts of others that I am holding on to." Then, still maintaining a ceremonial space, tear the paper into strips, one name to a strip, and burn each strip of paper. As each strip burns, visualize, imagine, feel, sense, and intuit the soul part being released from you and returning to the person. After each name has burned, you may want to make an offering to the spirits to thank them. You can add a pinch of cedar or sage to the fire. The act of releasing and returning the life-force energy of others brings with it a sense of completion and a general feeling of satisfaction. To use a metaphor, it is like finishing a chapter in your life.

After completing the ceremony, it is still possible over a period of time to recall additional names, faces, incidents, and so on. This is normal. You have opened the door to these submerged memories. The fire ceremony can be repeated at any time.

It really does take courage to embark on a journey to heal our deep wounding. It is the great journey of the soul, its desire to be whole again. One of the great gifts of our age is that this ancient wisdom is available to those who reach out for the joy and freedom of being their authentic selves. Clearly there has been a paradigm shift, an evolution in consciousness, an awakening since the 1960s that has created a new zeitgeist, and soul retrieval is a strong medicine for our times.

# 6

# YOUR REALITY IS SACROSANCT

*The cost of sanity, in this society, is a certain level of alienation.*

TERENCE MCKENNA

When I started to revise this book, there were many deletions, expansions, amendments, restructurings, and tweaks; this is a critical element of writing. Yet when I read this chapter it was metaphorically like sucking on a lemon. It was not that the writing or material was poor; it just did not flow with the book. I deleted the contents and paused to reflect: What do I want to say? What theme is close to my heart?

The following day, in an interesting synchronicity, while enjoying lunch with friends, the conversation turned to healing. A friend spoke about his mother, who had suffered a stroke and was immobilized in the hospital. The doctor said that she would never be able to move again, but despite this my friend gave his mother a gentle massage and sent healing energy to her. Gradually her body responded, and she started to move her arms, hands, and head. As this was happening the doctor walked in the room, and seeing this he said, "You are wasting your time. She can never move again." My friend's mother, on hearing the doctor, immediately slumped back into bed, became immobile, and unfortunately remained that way. His prognosis had proven to be correct. It was a classic *nocebo* (Latin for "I shall harm"), or effectively a curse.

After hearing this story, I knew what I wanted to write about, what was indeed close to my heart, something that was precious to me. We face these challenges daily, the challenges of honoring who we are, our cognitive freedom, and our personal integrity. Our enemies are legion.

Yes, I am indeed passionate about this, and of course there is a story. Please note that I have changed all the names in this narrative. Carmen, a young woman who required a wheelchair to get around, had been diagnosed with a form of muscular dystrophy. She enthusiastically participated in some of my workshops and even joined us on a group trip to Peru, where her profound heart's desire was to go to ancient site Machu Picchu. We brought her there, and although she was unable to move around in the vast site itself because of the steps and narrow paths, we got her settled in a sheltered place that offered a magnificent panoramic vista of the entire location. She was overjoyed, and it was a heartwarming experience for me to see that. I later went back to see how she was, and it was wonderful that she was still so thrilled about it.

A year later she came on a group trip to the Philippines to work with the psychic (bare hand) surgeons. She underwent a lot of operations with the healer Brother Roger, and a great deal was cleared from her body. Each day she became lighter and more flexible, her movements became supple and fluid, and she started to walk much more, albeit with a walking stick. A few months later at a workshop in the United Kingdom, I saw her again. She was transformed, and at one moment she threw away her walking stick and started to dance, to the great delight of everyone present.

Unfortunately, this rhapsodically beautiful story came to an end.

During the trip to the Philippines, Bert, one of the participants, developed a romance with Angel, a close friend of Grace, the healer's wife. He brought Angel back to England with him, where they married. However, Angel and Grace had an argument. This dispute became increasingly vindictive and spiteful, and Angel malevolently said to Bert that all the healing they received in the Philippines was a fake and that Brother Roger was a charlatan. This was done in a resentful and vengeful way to damage her antagonist. Bert took this in, and not believing the evidence of his own eyes or the huge benefits that he had received from working with the healer, he called Carmen and passed this on to her.

The outcome was devastating. Carmen lost her belief in her improvement, and slowly but surely she atrophied back into her former condition. Her heart was broken by this, and she was back in her wheelchair. Tragically, she passed away a few months after this. I was very upset and angry about this sordid affair caused by Angel and Bert, and I admit it took me many years to let go of my indignation and fury. As a postscript, the marriage between Bert and Angel did not last long at all. She soon left him for a wealthier man, but by that time I was not interested in the slightest in their drama. The destruction of a wonderful woman was their shameful legacy.

Words are powerful, but why? It is because they shape one's beliefs. Inner beliefs hold the real power. Inner beliefs are referred to as *unconscious* or *subconscious* beliefs, and if the words one uses resonate with an inner belief, those words will certainly have an effect. The first dictionary definition for *belief* runs along the lines of the following:

"An acceptance that something exists or is true, especially one without proof."[1]

We can tell ourselves that we believe in this or that, and if we do not open our minds to the possibility of modifying or changing a belief, it becomes a conviction that requires no actual evidence.

We all hold deep inner beliefs, and they may differ from our rational mind beliefs. If so, the inner beliefs will dominate in the long term. This is the reason why affirmations often do not work. People can stand in front of a mirror and say, "Every day and in every way I become more attractive and increasingly slender." Yet if this affirmation conflicts with an inner belief or conviction, such as when they were young they were told they were not much to look at or overweight, any success with the affirmation will only be temporary, if that. Affirmations and similar practices only address the conscious, rational mind. Inner beliefs are in our minds, in our bodies, and in our biogeometric energy field. In the first creative enrichment practice in chapter 12, I describe a practice that explores this very concept, a three-dimensional affirmation that includes our mind, body, and energy field.

The effects known as nocebo and *placebo* (Latin for "I shall please") illustrate the power of our beliefs. The latter has been studied intensively and is used as a control in pharmaceutical trials. A placebo is typically a sham medication or medical procedure that can nevertheless have a positive effect on a person, bringing tangible relief to pain or illness, even though the medicine is totally inert. It is the person's inner belief that the medicine or treatment will work that brings about the improvement in the health condition.

Dr. Bernard Lown, the world-renowned cardiologist and holder of the Nobel Peace Prize, writes in his book *The Lost Art of Healing* that the major problem in the practice of medicine is the interpersonal relationship between the doctor and patient. This relationship has been neglected in favor of reliance on technology and pharmaceutical solutions. He says, "Healing is best accomplished when art and science are conjoined, when body and spirit are probed together."[2] In this important book, he carefully describes the use of sympathetic listening and the influence of language on the patient's perception of the illness.

He advocates a holistic approach that also incorporates the latest medical technology and science harnessed together with compassion and the recognition that people are not just biological automatons.

## EXERCISE

### ✳ Rational Beliefs vs. Inner Beliefs

Let's briefly look at our rational mind beliefs and whether they are in sympathy with our inner beliefs. All that is required to do this exercise is your body, a pen, and a sheet of paper. The beautiful simplicity about our bodies is that they cannot lie, deceive, dissemble, or beguile us. So find somewhere comfortable where you will not be disturbed for twenty minutes. Once you are settled and relaxed, write down five of your core beliefs. They do not have to be about you. Some examples are:

- The Chicago Cubs will win the next World Series.
- I am an attractive and interesting person.
- I love myself.
- I am happy in my marriage.
- The government has our best interests at heart.

Having made your list, speak out loud a belief and then close your eyes and listen, feel, and sense your body's reaction. If you feel even the slightest sinking sensation, weight in your abdomen, tightness in your chest area, or any sense of your body folding in or shrinking, then you know without a doubt that your inner belief is not in line with your stated belief.

This relatively straightforward technique forms part of the body of practice used in traditional Chinese medicine (TCM), although TCM pays far more attention to subtle fluctuations in the flow of *chi,* or the human energy field. The same principle, based on TCM, is used in modern modalities such as applied kinesiology and Touch for Health.

We are manipulated through ingenious corporate strategies using the latest techniques in advertising and psychology to *desire* certain products or services. Although propaganda is as ancient as civilization itself, it has taken on a new force with the ubiquitous power of modern technology. This enhanced form of reality manipulation is used to influence us regarding the most trivial to the most momentous situations, and these persuasive techniques have far-reaching effects on the human condition.

To illustrate the trivial, I go into Starbucks or a similar coffee shop to order my usual black Americano coffee. As I stand at the counter, I am eye level with a wraparound display of enticing, delicious, scrumptious, appealing cakes, pastries, and croissants, which not only look lovely but also have a delectable "fresh-baked" aroma. Am I tempted? For sure I am. So there I am standing there with my mouth watering, considering adding a luscious cake to my order, until the inevitable and always innocently put question by the counter person: "Would you like anything more?" I think, "Here we go again." If only they had said nothing, maybe I would have ordered a cake, so I brusquely reply, "No, thank you. Just the coffee." This kind of selling technique is a bit too Pavlovian for my taste.

Small, pocket-size products in their shiny and colorful packaging are always on display at the supermarket check-out counter. It is just another way, albeit passively, to manipulate our reality. Language is also part of this. When you see platitudes along the lines of "we are here to help you" and "we are here to serve you," these cynical statements actually mean "we are here to make it easy for you to spend your money."

This is the battle we all face, to be strong and prevent another person or organization from distorting, twisting, and negating our experience, to be certain of our own reality. This struggle is ubiquitous and takes place on a social, a national, and a personal scale. As an example of manipulation that has grave and consequential repercussions, this harrowing sentiment was expressed at the Nuremburg war crime trials by Herman Goering. He is one of the most reviled and detested figures of the twentieth century, a man who was involved in the most abominable example of genocide in human history. He said:

> Naturally the common people don't want war, neither in Russia, nor in England, nor for that matter in Germany. That is understood. But, after all, it is the leaders of the country who determine the

policy and it is always a simple matter to drag the people along, whether it is a democracy, or a fascist dictatorship, or a parliament, or a communist dictatorship. Voice or no voice, the people can always be brought to the bidding of the leaders. That is easy. All you have to do is tell them they are being attacked, and denounce the peacemakers for lack of patriotism and exposing the country to danger. It works the same in any country.[3*]

What he said remains to this day lamentably valid, and the fact that this was expressed by Goering should make us all feel very uneasy indeed. You only have to look at the never-ending War on Terror or the Iraq war to unseat Saddam Hussein because he possessed weapons of mass destruction (WMD). We were told unequivocally that his WMD could be deployed within forty-five minutes and were aimed at European countries. All these claims were subsequently proven to be a misrepresentation of the facts, in fact, bare-faced lies. Yet this type of gross deception goes on and on, just the names of the countries change. However, if this approach fails, there is always the well-trod tirade, "If you are not with us, you are against us." This was taken to new and dazzling heights by George W. Bush: "Either you are with us, or you are with the terrorists."[4]

This statement and its insidious variations force people into a non-negotiable position. If you are not "with us," you are, by definition, an enemy. No room is allowed to accommodate a neutral, unaligned, or disinterested position. This is an example of gangster-style, brute-force reality distortion and manipulation. You are put in a position in which you have no discretion to choose; you *must* think and act in a certain way; otherwise, *your goose is going to be cooked.*

This manipulation occurs at every level. We have been effectively conditioned to believe that our bodies are not right. We have been

---

*This statement by Goering was recorded in Gustave Gilbert's transcriptions of conversations with him and many of the Nazi leaders during the Nuremberg War Crimes tribunal.

convinced, for example, that something is fundamentally wrong with our natural human body odor. Hundreds of millions of people deal with their perspiring armpit situation by spraying antiperspirants or applying roll-on products, many of which contain toxic substances such as aluminum. And by the way, this toxic metal is increasingly regarded as a causal factor in dementia. In this "there is something wrong about you" paradigm, our very identity, our gender is also a target. Intimate feminine deodorants often marketed with wonderful names evoking freedom, spiritual liberation, and magical sojourns in tropical paradises have been around for a long time. Even my testicles are also up for grabs, so to speak, with new products, one aptly named Fresh Balls. The deodorant trade is valued annually at billions of U.S. dollars, and they have successfully executed a phenomenal and indeed masterful act in the manipulation of our reality.

In 1951, psychologist Solomon Asch conducted a series of experiments in social psychology about conformity in group situations. These experiments were set up to investigate how social pressure could influence an individual to conform to a group. While most of the group knew this to be the purpose, one participant did not, and in fact that person understood that the purpose was to test visual abilities. The group was asked to determine the lengths of lines of differing sizes. The participants who were "in" on the purpose unanimously gave the wrong answers to the tests, leaving the sole uninformed participant in a quandary. Eventually doubting the evidence of his own eyes and his cognitive faculty, he sided with the majority. Ask yourself this question: Do I go along with the majority, or do I trust the evidence of my own eyes? It is something worth considering.

I have been giving both trivial and nontrivial examples because it is all a part of the same cloth. The perfidious doctrine of original sin, one of the foundational myths of Christendom, states that we are born bad, unacceptable, and undesirable; it provides the fabric into which all of these manipulative threads are woven. It is the legendary poison chalice that we have collectively drunk from.

It is easier to deconstruct and reconstruct a person's reality when that person is young. St. Ignatius of Loyola, founder of the Society of Jesus (Jesuits), reputedly said, "Give me the child till the age of seven, and I will show you the man."

At eleven years old, in the first music lesson at my new school, we all had to form a line and sing a note as the music teacher, Mr. Reid, walked by and listened. As it came to my turn, I opened my mouth to sing a note, but before the note had finished, he said, "Enough," and moved to the next in the line. That note never came out. It metaphorically got stuck in my throat, and I never sang in public again. I was ashamed of my own singing voice, and only many years later when I was chanting at ceremonies did I decide to do something to address this messy situation. I made an appointment with a music coach, and during the first session he listened to my singing and said that I have a good baritone voice. He sat at his piano and played while we both sang. There came a moment when our voices were in perfect harmony, and it was a sublime experience, a moment of euphoria. My voice sounded beautiful, my heart suddenly opened, and I burst into tears. The long-standing nocebo had been released, and I could sing again. In fact, at workshops people even ask me to sing.

We need to guard our cognitive faculties. Certain mind technologies are designed to influence the subconscious, thereby altering reality. In a therapeutic setting this is well and good. Hypnotherapy, Milton Erickson's work, and neurolinguistics programing (NLP) can often help in changing nonbeneficial behaviors. This is the contract that you and the therapist have made. However, be aware that these techniques are often used outside a consensual therapeutic environment. This entails a person using or mirroring your words to enter your conscious mind and then reframing the very terminology you use, consequently distorting your inner meaning and exercising control. If someone starts to mirror either your body posture or your words, it is time to sound an inner *Star Trek*-style red alert.

Plate 1. Detail from the painting *Concentración Palistica,*
by Pablo Amaringo

Plate 2. Traditional Andean curandera Doris Rivera Lenz and the author
at an *ofrenda* (offering) ceremony in Peru (Photo by Peter Cloudsley)

Plate 3. The feathers I use for shamanic extraction alongside the box I use to contain them. The feathers keep fresh and free of mites if stored in a box made of pine or a similar resinous, aromatic wood. (Photo by author)

Plate 4. Shaman Javier Arevalo shows encantos he uses in his healing work. (Photo by author)

Plate 5. This piece combines embroidery and traditional painting on white cotton. The paint is the dye made from crushing huito berries, and the white cotton is dyed with mahogany bark. (Photo by author)

Plate 6. Painting traditional Shipibo geometric designs on white cotton using huito berry dye (Photo by author)

Plate 7. Painting on white cotton made with dye from the huito berry (*Genipa americana*). The zigzag motif around the edges is symbolic of Ronin, the cosmic anaconda. This type of traditional textile painting is called a *chupa*. (Photo by author)

Plate 8. *The Geometry of an Arkana* by Howard G. Charing. Compare with facing plate 9.

Plate 10. My tambo at Mishana on the Rio Nanay (Photo by author)

Plate 9. Cymatic photo of the sound emitted by a Tibetan singing bowl called the Great Star Mother Bowl (Photo by John Stuart Reid, © by Frank Perry)

Plate 11. A cataract is visible spread on the side of the glass. (Photo by Patrick Hamouy)

Plate 12. The six creative enrichment practices, mapped onto the ancient Flower of Life symbol from sacred geometry, which is a visual expression of the underlying geometric structure of creation

1. Align the mind-body system with the universal creative source.
2. Dissolve the inner obstacles to creativity.
3. Encounter the archetype of primordial creativity.
4. See the world like a child again.
5. Discover the luminous symbol of your creative power.
6. Manifest your creative energy.

Another reality-distortion method is to reply to something you have just said with "Are you sure?" or "Really?" Or someone might repeat what you have just said but in a different way, using similar but subtly nuanced words, and this twisted verbal exchange can continue until you have finally said what he or she wanted you to say. This gives the other person the advantage or leverage he or she intended. The original meaning of what you said has become distorted. Do you know people who do that?

Another way our reality is challenged is when people are in denial either of an action they have taken or of something they have said. When you say to them that you disagree with what they did or said, they will deny it. So you are faced with a tough choice, either to deny the evidence of your own senses or to accept the imposition of *their* version of reality. This is where the term *mind fuck* is appropriate. If you do the latter and allow them to impose their reality over yours, then you have certainly compromised your experience, your cognitive faculties, and, above all, your soul. When this happens to me, as it does on occasion, and even though it can mean the end of an old friendship, the choice is clear. I will not distort or compromise my reality or my soul, *regardless of the consequences,* and I mean that 100 percent. From a philosophical and spiritual standpoint, these situations come up so you can learn and evolve, and thereby become a stronger person. It is the challenge of the soul warrior.

Many who are on a spiritual or shamanic path experience extrasensory encounters with spiritual forces, communion with angels, or even communication with a departed loved one. At times this can be truly heartwarming and transformative. People who have spoken to me about this happily concede that they have experienced out of the ordinary experiences but are usually reluctant to share them, concerned about what other people might think.

Here we address the question of what is real and what is not. It is such a damned hard question, one that has been probed, examined, investigated, and scrutinized by scientists, philosophers, and theologians over the course of countless years. Now, according to the current arbiters of our reality—psychiatrists—nonordinary, spiritual experiences are not real at all; they are hallucinations. In this book I have described some of my experiences, and I am sure that a psychiatrist would diagnose auditory, kinesthetic, and visionary hallucinatory psychosis.

Dr. Oliver Sacks, the renowned psychiatrist and author, in his fascinating book *Hallucinations* goes into this in great detail both anecdotally and theoretically. It is not a clinical book by any means. He describes with compassion his interaction and correspondence with patients. In one of the chapters, titled "Hearing Things," he describes an experience in which he was in mortal danger while trying to descend a mountain with a badly injured leg. At his most despondent moment in this crisis, he heard a forceful and commanding voice that gave him specific instructions that not only gave him the resolution and courage to continue but also enabled him to get to safety. He describes this not as a nonordinary encounter, but as an *auditory hallucination,* a psychosis associated perhaps with abnormal activity of the primary auditory cortex. I was not convinced that Dr. Sacks in his heart truly meant this. Maybe he had to qualify it as a hallucinatory experience because of his professional demands, but I certainly read between the lines a hint of cognitive dissonance.

Many friends and clients have had an encounter with a warm, encouraging, and compassionate presence or voice at defining moments in their lives. One instance for me took place shortly after my father died in 1991. I was feeling forlorn regarding my marriage. I felt so strongly that I had to separate from Shelley. This was not about her—we remain to this day close friends; rather, it was a *calling* from my soul. I had to embark on a new journey in life, leave my existing world, and travel into uncharted territory. This calling clashed with my deep-seated conviction that marriage was for life. At this defining moment, when I was staring into the abyss, my father appeared. My dad had remarkably large hands, and I felt his large hand on my shoulder as if consoling me. I could smell his distinct body odor, and then he leaned down and spoke in my ear, "It is okay son. You can do what you need to do." It was his voice, his words, and of course he is the only man who can authentically call me "son." It was an incredibly moving moment for me. My dad, who in life was warm-hearted and gentle, had in spirit come to me in my hour of great despair. He gave me permission to separate. To this day, I am not sure if I could have had the courage to end my marriage if it was not for his intervention. Why would I want to classify this sublime experience as abnormal auditory, olfactory, and visual activity in my brain chemistry when in my soul I know it was real?

Reality is subjective; so never allow your reality to be undermined. Your reality is truly sacrosanct; at the end of the day it is all we have. I am reminded of the biblical story in Genesis of Esau selling his birthright (inheritance) to Jacob for a bowl of soup. That is what we figuratively do; that is what we are manipulated to do. Be aware; have confidence in who you are and what you do. Never compromise your bliss and do not sell or give away your birthright.

# 7

# THE CONTINUUM OF LIFE

*We often wonder: "How will I be when I die?" The answer to that is that whatever state of mind we are in now, whatever kind of person we are now, that's what we will be like at the moment of death, if we do not change. This is why it is so absolutely important to use this lifetime to purify our mind-stream, and so our basic being and character, while we can.*

SOGYAL RINPOCHE

In our culture, death is regarded as dark, mysterious, and fearful. In many respects, discussing death and dying is not only regarded as morbid but also as taboo. Of course, the paradox is that death is the single experience that will happen with undeniable certainty to each and every one of us. Typically, we skirt the matter until one day we come face to face with this quintessential personal and inevitable circumstance. Ancient cultures did not regard death as an enemy, but rather dared to make it an ally.

How we experience death is in many ways dependent on how we live our lives. Sogyal Rinpoche, author of the book *The Tibetan Book of Living and Dying,* puts it succinctly, "Death is like a mirror in which the true meaning of life is reflected."[1]

Those who have had near-death experiences invariably regard this singular experience as a transformative event in their lives. The common thread of these experiences is gaining the awareness that life, albeit in another form, continues.

So this is the essential core of the teachings about death in many spiritual traditions. It is primarily about life and how we can intensify the experience, bringing meaning and purpose into our life. Just the awareness that death does not signify the end of consciousness but is more of a passage in an incalculably vast journey offers a profound serenity and peace of mind.

It is ultimately about daring to live fearlessly from the center of one's truth, to challenge and defeat the tendency to inertia, fear of life, and premature old age. In the words of the Peruvian shaman Don Eduardo Calderon, "A shaman is someone who is already dead and thus has no fear of death or life."[2] Sometimes a life-threatening crisis is what calls a person to the way of the shaman. From this perspective, death is not perceived as the enemy of life. The real adversary is inertia.

I have faced imminent death twice in my life. *I knew that I was going to die.* Both of these events irrevocably changed my life. The first was the elevator crash, and the second was so sublime, it was my greatest test. I faced my greatest fear, not of death but of oblivion, and it was my greatest healing.

I was also born dead; I remember my actual birth and the very first words spoken. I was presumed dead, so the surgeon performed the procedure to remove a dead fetus by Caesarean section. After I was extracted and obviously not dead, he said in astonishment, "It's alive!" I also recalled the particular smell of the maternity room; it had the distasteful pungent odor of the old type of oil solvent-based gloss paint. When I asked my mother about my birth, she was stunned. "How do you know?" Yet she verified everything and felt comfortable in telling me more about the circumstances surrounding my birth. She also added that the operating theater had just been repainted and had an overpowering stench.

According to medical science, this memory is not possible, as the cerebral cortex (the specific part of the brain that stores permanent memories) is not yet formed at birth. From the matter-creates-mind materialistic paradigm, it is simply out of the question. So how could I remember my birth? *Where* was I at the time? The memories and life experience, as I proposed earlier, are not stored in the physical brain; they are part of the soul fabric, the fibers and filaments that form our biogeometric structure. The analogy that the brain functions as a television receiver that decodes invisible electromagnetic signals into a visible image is crude and reinforces the notion of a fragmented reality. The brain-consciousness connection is a *synergism,* the product of an interaction between different systems that together create a whole greater than the sum of their individual parts. This is a *holistic* perspective, as opposed to the dualistic view that human consciousness and the cosmos are separate. This is the enduring ontological question: Did consciousness exist before matter such that matter extends from consciousness, or does matter produce consciousness? The latter is the predominant view of the reductionist Cartesian view that pervades medical science to an extent that the whole of the body system is fragmented into distinct specializations, such as endocrinology, cardiology, gastroenterology, gynecology, hepatology, and so on. Holistic practitioners and shamans view the physical, emotional, and mental spheres not as discrete compartmentalized systems, but as an integral whole. So how did the reductionist worldview arise?

On the night of November 10, 1619, the French philosopher René Descartes, then a mercenary soldier, had a dream during the siege of Ulm in Germany during the Thirty Years' War. As he described in his journal, a giant winged angel appeared and said, "The conquest of nature is to be achieved through measure and number."[3] This message transformed his life and led him to develop the rationalist philosophy now known as Cartesian dualism. This is the concept that body and mind are separate and that human beings—and all natural phenomena—are merely physical entities. In this philosophy, consciousness is an irrelevant, superfluous concept. Of course, the great paradox is that modern science stems from the intervention of a *supernatural* being.

This dualistic perspective is prevalent in our thinking. I watched the brilliant BBC documentary "The Hidden Life of the Cell" in the series *Our Secret Universe.* In the past ten years, scientists have been able to witness what once seemed impossible: the world inside a human cell. Professor Steve Jones of University College in London, who introduced the program, said, "When I was a student, the idea that we could burrow deep inside a human cell was unthinkable. The more we learn about the universe the simpler it seems, but the cell isn't like that. The more we find out the more complicated things get." I thought, "That's interesting. . . . This implies that the human cell is not a part of the universe."

In traditional wisdom and knowledge, life is a continuum that does not end at the moment of death. One of the most important traditional tasks of the seer, shaman, or medicine man or woman is to assist either people who are dying or the spirits of those who have died to make the transition into the Great Domain of consciousness. This body of practice is known as *psychopomp work,* from the Greek word *psychopompos,* which literally means "conductor of souls." In Greek mythology, the god Hermes served as the escort for the dead into the afterlife. This concept of a guide or intermediary between the living and the dead is a collective theme found in most religions, spiritual traditions, and mythologies.

Sogyal Rinpoche, in *The Tibetan Book of Living and Dying,* reveals a deep understanding of the cosmology in which we live. An essential part of Tibetan spirituality is the state of awareness at the boundary of life and death.

## ONCE UPON A TIME

We live knowing of the certainty of our death. Would knowledge of our death teach us how to transform our life in the present? This is not as far-fetched as it may seem. In the last one hundred years, our understanding of the very nature of *time* has undergone a revolution, introducing a totally new scientific, philosophical, and spiritual paradigm. Time for Newton was an inherent constant of the universe, and he knew that time always changes at the same rate for everyone, everywhere.

For us, time, like a river, seems to flow in one direction, always toward the future. But according to physics such may not be the case. Einstein explored the concept of time and discovered the profound link between space and time. Einstein, with his theory of special relativity, unified the idea of space and time into a four-dimensional structure called *spacetime*. With this profound insight, he forever transformed how we see time. The flow of time, which appears to us as real as the flow of a river, may be nothing more than an illusion. "The distinction between past, present, and future," Einstein writes, "is only a stubbornly persistent illusion."[4] Past, present, and future may all exist in a single infinitely indescribable moment.

What if . . . we could transport or extend our consciousness to the point of our death? What would we learn from this, the greatest of mysteries? Is it possible that this revelation has the potential to transform our lives? One of the underlying precepts of the shamanic journey is that human perception extends beyond the reach of the senses. The practitioner journeys outside of linear sequential time. This is the principle behind soul retrieval, the psychopomp, and divination. I consider, and this is just my opinion, that it if we embraced the notion of our death as an advisor we would gain a transcendent insight with *transformational* potential. A shamanic journey or a deep meditation can bestow the revelatory knowledge of how we will die, and the wisdom to guide us to change our life if our death is not auspicious.

The following account tells what happened to me when on a

shamanic journey in which a Tibetan lama spirit guide appeared and spoke to me. I was doing a simultaneous narration into my tape recorder so I could later transcribe the journey. I find that this is a useful practice, as subtle elements of a journey can be overlooked on returning to everyday consciousness. This is what he said:

*"Howard, why do you dice with death? Be at peace with your own death; allow things to flow through you; rise above them."*

*"How?" I ask.*

*"Look upon the true reason of life, meditate upon existence, merge with the reality that is the human spirit, and surrender to the will of that divine nature. Be as the wind: uncontained, grace and movement combined, with gentleness and strength as its nature. It is contained in nothing, yet contains much; it is the nature of wind to sustain life in its purest form, for it holds in it the very element of life.*

*"The time of the old teachings has come and gone. Humanity finds itself in such a state of disquiet, disease, and self-sabotage that even the wind must rally itself into a force that can be felt, a force that in its wake will sweep up the debris.*

*"Humans have come to a nexus point, a point of no return, and fear itself holds back our evolution. Those who can stop it must do so now, must speak out, must act and live the life of a humanitarian and be like the wind, blasting a path through that fear and taking humankind into the state of its true being, for without the true willingness of those who can, humankind will be no more."*

*I was shown an image of a candle being extinguished.*

*"Howard, be compassionate with yourself, love the humanity within you, and forgive yourself for your procrastination. Turn your eyes toward peace and God, put yourself aside, and, like me, do your job. Buddha needs a lotus flower on which to rest. Why is it that on seeing the lotus flower, you will not rest within its petals? And why, when it is requested of you to be the lotus flower, do you close your leaves and petals and sink beneath the water? Love is the resting place. Be open and receive it.*

*"The wind exists for itself, and it exists for humanity. You cannot lose your identity, and yet you have such a fear of beauty and gentleness."*

*I saw the image of a lotus flower of light, with humankind resting on it. The guide continued: "The water is absolute calm, and love rests upon calm emotions. The water is so deep, and there is love and compassion. The lotus flower is the cradle, Buddha resting, being at peace.*

*"The lotus flower stops Buddha from sinking into the emotions, and love stops Buddha from sinking into the depths. Simplicity is the key to the human heart, for within it, there is no room for confusion. Confusion creates a state of fear, which closes down the portals.*

*"Why do you dice with death?*

*"Why do you seek to purge yourself of that which you are in order to become that which you already are?*

*"Howard, live a life to prepare for a peaceful death."*

I then witnessed my own death. I won't go into the details, but it was a good death.

This journey has continued to be an exquisite inspiration for my life. It offers the great teaching that to realize a peaceful death, I need to live a peaceful life.

Please note, I am not suggesting that you should or need to journey to your final moment on Earth, and certainly not to the exact day or time, as that could generate anxiety, and worse, it could become a self-fulfilling prophecy.

Here is a way to see this journey of discovery. Do not ask: What did I achieve in my life? What were my failures? What were the things that I wanted to do but never did? That is the rational mind and transient ego speaking. Remember, this is a journey of the soul and ask instead: What is the feeling in my heart? Stay with any sadness you feel, follow the threads of those feelings back in time, and allow the inner stories to emerge and illuminate yourself in the here and now.

Later, allow the realizations to filter through: What should I have done? What did I not complete? What have I learned from these insights? How can I change my life to be at peace?

This is the power of *farseeing,* which means accessing visionary prescient knowledge that has the potential to benignly influence the present.

## PREBIRTH EXISTENCE

As a child, I was fascinated with the actuality of being alive. This sense of wonder has never fully gone away. Even now, if I reflect on it, I still have the feeling that it is wonderfully weird to be alive. In the late 1980s I was drawn to the work of John-Richard Turner, who developed the *prebirth matrix.* This method takes you back to the precise moment of your conception, when you became aware. That moment holds the emotional blueprints, the source of the prevalent emotional patterns experienced in life. I attended the trainings, conferences, and seminars, eventually becoming a qualified practitioner of this body of work. It did indeed open many doors to awakening the memories of my birth, as I have previously mentioned, and also intriguingly the time before my birth.

We inherit not only the biological genetic coding of our parents but also their mental and emotional states during the nine months prior to our birth. With this knowledge, deep transformational growth can happen, transmuting negative, diminishing thoughts and self-judgments into qualities that enhance our well-being and life. I still offer workshops on the prebirth body of practices as they clearly help people to discover and heal the underlying emotional patterns that create dissatisfaction and unhappiness in their lives. This body of work is particularly beneficial in identifying and releasing the emotional impediments that prevent people from enjoying intimate and meaningful relationships.

In addition to the growth of our physical body in the womb, we also experience the development of our emotional and mental body, and these stem from our mother's energy body. John-Richard Turner called this *emotional DNA* (eDNA). The developing fetus experiences the mother's thoughts and feelings, and those become the emotional basis for the child's life.

At the time this concept was put forth, we did not have any scientific data for it, although there was a significant body of anecdotal evidence. However, that has all changed with the amazing discovery of epigenetics. The eminent geneticist Professor Marcus Pembrey introduces the idea that the lives of our parents, grandparents, and previous generations can directly affect our well-being, despite never experiencing any of the things they experienced.

One of the firmest tenets of biology is that at the moment of our conception, we receive a set of chromosomes from our mother and father, and that DNA genetic coding is immutable. Our genes remain intact and unaffected either by the way we live or by our environmental conditions. The Human Genome Project started in the early 1990s with the objective to map the entire human genetic code, the biological blueprint for humans. This blueprint would offer a complete understanding of our biology at the molecular level, with the promise that scientists could find the genetic cause and cure for every disease. We could follow this map to biological utopia.

This utopia was never achieved because they realized that the number of human genes was considerably less than the original assumption of about one hundred thousand genes; in fact, the human genome is less complex than and has fewer genes than plants. The current assumption is that there are fewer than thirty thousand genes. This discovery led scientists to the conclusion that gene studies provide no way to explain the complexity of the human organism. There is clearly more to inheritance than the basic DNA sequence. Something other than DNA mediates biological inheritance, an elusive *meta-agent* that controls the function of our genes. It means that biological inheritance is not simply based on the genes that you inherit but on the internal configuration of the genes. This implies the existence of an independent genetic substratum that modifies the genes.

"We realized that we were dealing with what is now known as genomic imprinting," says Professor Pembrey. "What genomic imprinting means is, in a nutshell, that genes have a *memory* of where they came from."[5]

I emphasized the word *memory* because that could refer to the meta-agent that informs our consciousness and physical form. We could call it *hypermemory* or eDNA, a means to transmit ancestral emotional experiences. This correlates with the holistic notion that consciousness existed before matter and that life, as the sages and philosophers have said, is a continuum. However, whether either can be proven or disproven is another story. The following discussion between two great minds, Carl Sagan and the Dalai Lama, took place in 1991. Sagan relates:

> In theological discussions with religious leaders, I often ask what their response would be if a central dogma of their faith were disproved by scientific discipline. When I put this question to the Dalai Lama, he unhesitatingly replied as no traditionalist or fundamentalist religious leaders do: In such a case, he said, Tibetan Buddhism would have to alter. Even, I asked, if it's a really central tenet, like reincarnation? Even then, he replied. However, he said mischievously—it will be hard to disprove reincarnation![6]

## EXERCISE

### ✖ Journey to the Moment of Your Conception

To look at our conception, the creation of our physical incarnation, we need to place it in a broader context. We are considering the eternal and immutable self, or soul, not the "I" of our present lifetime. Our incarnation is not a result of chance or luck; it is karmic. This incarnation is but one step in the soul's evolution, its ongoing development and illumination, and one of the goals is to resolve unfinished patterns that were experienced in past lives. When we die in a past life with unresolved, diminishing emotional and mental patterns, our consciousness seeks the opportunity to transform and release these unresolved patterns. This is nonjudgmental and beyond the dualistic notion of "good" or "bad." In order to release these patterns, we need to be in the physical world and enter into a set of circumstances that will allow us to activate them.

In this vast and timeless field of consciousness, we are energetically drawn to our predestined mother and father, who themselves are resonating with the same emotional and mental frequencies that we experienced in a past life. This mutual soul resonance draws us to our parents' consciousness.

In this journey you will gain insight into some of your most deeply seated emotional patterns. This journey is based on the initial section of the prebirth matrix. You can try this practice by using a meditation practice or by using a shamanic journey. For clarity, the narrative is in the first person.

I allow myself to be aware of the consciousness of my father, how he is feeling within himself, about himself at the moment of making love, an act that will result in my conception.

I ask myself: "Are the emotions that Father was experiencing familiar feelings in my life?"

I allow myself to be aware of the feelings that Father is having at this time about Mother.

I ask myself: "Do the feelings that Father was having toward Mother appear as familiar relationship patterns in my life?"

I allow myself to be aware of the consciousness of Mother, how she is feeling at the moment of making love, an act that will result in my conception.

I ask myself: "Are the emotions that Mother was experiencing familiar feelings in my life?"

I allow myself to be aware of the feelings that Mother is having at this time toward Father.

I ask myself: "Do the feelings that Mother was having toward Father appear as familiar relationship patterns in my life?"

In the act of making love, hundreds of millions of sperm are released. From this multitude only a single sperm will be successful and fertilize the egg.

I allow myself to be aware of the consciousness of that single sperm, that one sperm that will fertilize the egg, an act that will result in my conception.

I ask myself: "What is my consciousness? What feelings is the sperm having? Are these familiar feelings in my life?"

And now I turn to Mother's egg, which since her birth has been fully formed in her ovary. It is now released and starts the journey into the fallopian tubes.

I ask myself: "What is her consciousness? What feelings is the egg having? Are these familiar feelings in my life?"

And now as the egg moves along the fallopian tube, it sees the approaching sperm for the first time.

I ask myself: "What is the egg's consciousness? What feelings is the egg having on seeing the approaching sperm for the first time? Are these familiar feelings in my life?"

And now, that single sperm sees the egg for the first time.

I ask myself: "What is the sperm's consciousness? What feelings is the sperm having on seeing the egg for the first time? Are these familiar feelings in my life?"

And now, I turn to the millions of sperm surrounding and engulfing the egg.

I ask myself: "What is the egg's consciousness? What feelings is the egg having at this moment? Are these familiar feelings in my life?"

Turn now to the moment just before conception, when the merging of the sperm and egg takes place.

I ask myself: "Where is my consciousness, my awareness of self at this moment?"

And now, the egg has opened its outer membrane and permits the single sperm to enter. The sperm and egg join, merge, and create a new form of life. This is the moment of conception, the beginning of life.

I ask myself: "What are my feelings at this moment? What unresolved emotional patterns are to be activated, experienced, and released?"

✖

When you have completed this journey, come back into everyday awareness. Record your observations and the associated feelings. Then I suggest that you put this information away until the following day and allow your awakened feelings, insights, and memories to organize into a cogent form during your sleep. The following day, review and ponder the material. Have you gained an insight into the emotional patterns in your life?

# 8

# ENERGY MEDICINE

## Exploring the Human Energy Field

*Ayahuasca has revealed to me that you need both light and darkness to be illuminated. In order to appreciate the spiritual nature of humanity and the prevalent cosmic forces, you must understand that the negative side is there to show you the positive side.**

PABLO AMARINGO

In chapter 3, I discussed how our psyche and senses operate as a single system to receive and interpret energy fields. This biogeometric energy field is a metalibrary of life stories that the person has experienced from the moment of conception.

At the start of a session, I do not ask my clients any questions. I am interested in their stories, but if they relate their life problems, tell me what is not working for them, and so on, it could influence or

---

*Pablo Amaringo discussing his painting titled *Puñusca Muscuna* (meaning "profound revelation" in the Quechua language). Quechua, the original language of the Andean civilizations, was not written down until the arrival of the missionaries and the conquistadors in the sixteenth century.

predispose my visionary interpretation, so I prefer to avoid that situation and start with a clean slate, that is, no prior information. Some of my clients are psychotherapists, and this is a novelty for them because they are predisposed to clients telling them about their circumstances.

In chapter 5, I described how I perceive the soul using the metaphor of a three-dimensional tapestry consisting of threads, fibers, and filaments. In this metaphor, each thread is a discrete element, a story or an experience that stretches back in time. Any traumatic event that took place in a person's life, no matter how early, will be discernible in that individual's field, as the following story illustrates.

One female client complained of a tight throat and difficulty in swallowing. She had seen doctors and other healers, and nothing seemed to help. As I attuned to her field, I immediately saw hands locked around her throat as if she was being strangled. I asked her if she in some way felt as if she was being strangled. She nodded yes, hardly able to speak.

I forced open the hands that were gripping her throat, and after this was accomplished, her face changed color and she started to breathe vigorously. I said that she had been strangled by a young man. She said her brother had tried to kill her in this way several years previously, and her sister had intervened to stop it. After the session, she felt relaxed, and her face looked much softer and not strained.

Later in the evening, after I sat down to read a newspaper, I became aware of a presence in the room. I looked closer and found it to be the brother of the client. I remembered that I had neglected to clear his energy body. It was late, and I had wound down, and this was the last thing that I wanted to do, but it needed to be done. As I started to get up from the chair, a glowing circle suddenly appeared up against the ceiling. The circle opened wider, and a large arm came out and seized the brother's energy body. It withdrew the body up into the glowing circle. I was very curious, so I stood underneath the glowing circle and looked up. Above me, I saw the Tibetan monks waving at me and smiling. The quality of the place behind the circle was different, luminous and shimmering with an iridescent light. As I moved closer to the spirit realm, it felt as if I was in a heavier and denser substance, like water, and it seemed as though I was looking up through the water into air. This was a revelation; I had a direct encounter with the vibrational boundary between the physical world and the spirit dimension.

I learned to be cautious working with the energy body after an experience attuning to a client back in 1993. I saw that he was impaled by a shaft of intense light. It did not appear to be natural, and as I reached out to touch it, I felt as if a bolt of electricity had hit my hand, leaving a circular indent in the palm (which is still there today). The client told me that he had recently had radiotherapy. I realized the shaft of light was the residuum of the radiation remaining in his energy field. He felt a lot better after it had been removed, but I felt terrible. I felt misaligned, unwell, fatigued, and unable to work. I went to see Harry Oldfield, an innovative scientist in England who has developed a fascinating technology that allows subtle energy fields to be imaged, realigned, and much more. He hooked me up to his PIP (polycontrast interference photography) device, and I could see on the screen that the energy field on my right side was barely discernible, while the energy on my left side appeared vibrant. This made total sense because my right hand had been injured. After the diagnosis, Harry used his electrocrystals device to rebalance my energy field. It worked a treat, and I felt well and vibrant again. For those who are interested in this technology, Harry provides detailed information on this science as well as photographs of human energy fields on his website.

## THE EFFECT OF ABORTIONS ON THE HUMAN ENERGY FIELD

Abortion continues to be a difficult personal matter as well as a challenging cultural issue. The argument of whether abortion should be permissible is, without a doubt, one of the most highly charged disputes waged across the political, legal, social, and religious arenas. I am not here to judge anyone. As an anarchistic antiauthoritarian individual, I hold the principle that it is a personal decision and that the state should not interfere in personal freedoms. Although I hold the view that a person's body belongs to that person, the state might disagree and believe that it belongs to the state. Regarding the term *abortion,* the medical terminology used is *termination*; this enables a woman to maintain some emotional distance from this demanding act.

In my work with women I can perceive the damage in their energy field when they have had an abortion; it is as if a part of them has died. I have only compassion for the woman because I am aware of the suffering and the powerful self-judgments made when struggling with the dilemma of whether to do this. Also, at times, the energy body of the fetus remains with the woman, and she may grieve for the loss at a deep intimate level. Even though the woman may have rationalized the act or suppressed the feelings, she may be experiencing sorrow, depression, a feeling of disconnection to life, a sense of emotional numbness, or the pervasive feeling that a part of her has died. These are symptoms of *soul loss,* and soul loss protects the person from being overwhelmed with emotional pain.

A soul retrieval can help the woman to release the pain and grief, which from a spiritual perspective is one of the hardest acts to do. A soul retrieval also provides an opportunity to release the soul of the unborn child for the healing and evolution of both beings. This is a beautiful and moving unbonding ceremony in which the energy body of the unborn child is presented to her. This is generally experienced tangibly as the woman enters into a perceptible communion while holding the essence of the unborn child. The energy body essence is transmuted by a spirit guide,* passes into the spirit world, and rejoins the Great Domain of infinite consciousness. I feel very privileged to be present at these moments of beauty and grace.

---

*When the energy is transmuted it is changed into a finer soul substance, a different vibration of energy that will allow the energy to return to a higher vibrational field.

Perhaps as a society we could look at ways to bridge this massive chasm between opposing views by restoring an element of spiritual awareness. Here is where we can benefit from the wisdom of the shamanic cultures. A first step could be to modify the nonemotive clinical terminology used by the medical profession that reinforces detachment from our intimate feelings. The parties involved could be encouraged and guided to perform a releasing and unbonding ceremony that acknowledges the departure of the unborn child. This ceremony would take place without any judgments, and the parents could forgive and bless both themselves and the unborn child. My personal sentiments are that an approach along these lines would relieve distress and bring comfort and closure.

A last thought on this matter: although I have discussed abortions, an unbonding ceremony is eminently appropriate for the loss caused by an abortion or a miscarriage as well. I can speak personally about the efficacy and value of releasing this grief.

### EXERCISE

## ✳ An Unbonding Ceremony

This ceremony is performed to release the pain and grief from a personal loss. Grieving for the loss of a loved one or for a deep relationship is probably one of the most raw and intense emotional experiences in our lives. The grief needs to flow through our being so we can release it, reclaim our lives, and move again into the beauty of our existence. It is difficult to release grief because we hold on to the memories and feelings of that time or person, but in doing this our life becomes clouded and we feel weighed down.

In this unbonding ceremony we give our pain to the higher order consciousness for transformation and release. The full moon is a powerful time for this ceremony. The moon in this phase symbolizes endings, transformation, and a new cycle of life. In shamanic traditions the mind and emotions are regarded as being in an open and awakened state at the time of the full moon. Buddha achieved his enlightenment and total freedom as the full moon rose after forty-nine days of meditation under the Bodhi Tree.

To prepare for the ceremony, you need to prepare a *giveaway,* an object that you craft or paint that provides an evocative symbol of your grief, words on paper that describe your feelings and memories about the loss, or a photograph that evokes deep-seated emotions regarding your loss. The important thing as you prepare the craft, note, or photo is to be conscious and aware of your grief and pain. This giveaway should be a profound and eloquent expression of your anguish and sorrow.

This ceremony is best conducted outdoors in nature. You will need your giveaway; a safe place to make a fire; and aromatic natural incense such as copal resin (*Protium copal*), white sage (*Salvia apiana*), or a stick of palo santo (*Bursera graveolens*). Feel free to include any items that embody a spiritual quality for you.

When you are ready, light the fire. While holding the giveaway, watch the flames as they rise and focus on their shapes, the shadows, the many colors and shades—the reds, the violets, and the yellows. In this way you can gently enter into a communion with the primal elemental spirit of fire. At a certain point you will feel the pull or an ineffable impulse to place the giveaway into the fire. As you do this, say the following words (or, of course, choose your own vocabulary):

> *Everything has its time to end*
> *Everything has its time to begin*
> *Now at the full moon is this time*
> *Where there has been a bonding, let there be an*
>     *unbonding for the benefit of all*
> *What I have been holding on to, I now release*
> *I now give this object to the elemental force of fire*
> *To transform and release my sorrow*
> *Now is the time for a new beginning*

Stay with the fire until the object has burned to ashes. You can collect the ashes and later place them into a body of flowing water, such as a river or the sea, while invoking the elemental force of water. Or scatter the ashes to the wind, invoking the elemental force of air. Conscious awareness while carrying out this ceremony will help you to release the sorrow and grief and start a new creative cycle in your life.

## IN THE LIGHT OR IN THE DARK?

Words are loaded with meaning. Light is often a synonym for *good,* and dark is a synonym for *bad.* We all have elements of the dark and the light within us. This interplay of energy is exemplified by the ancient concept of yin and yang, which describes that totality is a dynamic flow, formed of opposite and seemingly contradictory forces. These forces, however, are actually complementary and interdependent. The yin/yang symbol illustrates that everything contains its opposite and that neither can exist without the other (figure 8.1).

The coexistence of the dark and the light within us is not a problem; rather, the challenge is which of these polarities we embrace and express. This is a classical theme, seen, for example, in the saga of Darth Vader, which continues to be a popular and existential parable of our times. His redemption when he makes the ultimate choice and rejects the "dark side" in favor of love is my über favorite scene from the *Star Wars* movies.

Figure 8.1. The yin/yang symbol

I touched my "dark side" some years ago when I became embroiled with an individual who practiced sorcery not only to gain power over other people but also as a conduit for his malevolence. I became aware of his machinations against me following a powerful ayahuasca session in which I became "transparent" and saw this nauseating and obnoxious energy within me. This foul and obscene energy released, and I felt much better, but I had worked myself up to an angry and indignant state. I was enraged that someone had tried to kill me, so I decided to retaliate and end the matter once and for all. I made my preparations to do this, and then I heard my Tibetan guide say, "Howard, do not do this thing. You will harm your soul, you will be like him; and if he dies because of this, you will take on his karma." The guide's voice was there all the time, yet in my indignation, I had just not heard him. I immediately cancelled the retaliation plan, just dropped the whole matter and forgave the person. When I had done that, the guide spoke again, this time a single word: "Good." I experienced great relief and felt in some way that I had passed a test. Then he spoke again. "Do not concern yourself any more with him; you are protected against his malicious endeavors," and so I was at peace with this.

One of the most important life lessons that I learned from this episode was that although I had been attacked by this repugnant energy, it only worked because there was a similar frequency within me; that was the hook, as you will manifest in your life what you are, what is within, either consciously or unconsciously. This situation was a teaching; it is always uncomfortable to look into the mirror and see your own unresolved mess. This was a clarion call to acknowledge these uncomfortable and raw aspects within my being and to ultimately accept responsibility for them and heal them. It was also a personal redemption, and maybe that is why the Darth Vader story resonates with me . . . just saying!

Anyhow, I learned much from this episode; it was a salutary reminder to be aware of the interplay between the dark and the light within me, and to always take the correct and impeccable path. I must never allow an inner wound to dictate my actions, and, yes, if I am hurt,

I must see this as an opportunity to seek healing and inner equilibrium. In many respects, this person has been a great teacher to me and has served my spiritual growth by revealing my own deficiencies, thereby offering me the opportunity to heal them. People do not care to admit that they have come close to crossing the moral line, and I am no different. I was inspired to disclose this story because the author Steve Beyer, a man of peace and conciliation, wrote in his book a section entitled "How I Became a Sorcerer." In this he describes an incident triggered by his offended ego and how he lost control. By writing this account, Steve has presented us with a beautiful gift, and for me it is an invitation to be open. We are all human, but in this work, self-control, introspection, and rigorous discipline are, without a doubt, an *absolute* imperative.

We all have to cope with unsavory negative situations in our everyday lives. People may open our wounds, put us down, and make snide, cutting comments that are very upsetting. In many New Age and shamanic circles, people advocate personal energetic protection strategies. Probably the most well-known examples are surrounding oneself with a shield of radiant white light or placing oneself in a protective "plastic" bubble and visualizing negative energy bouncing off the protective bubble. I think that such strategies can benefit many people, and I also add that communication between people consists of more than just words alone. We receive energy (negative and positive) with our solar plexus, and that is why when dealing with a negative person, it feels that we have been punched in our stomach. Placing your attention on your solar plexus, or even covering up your solar plexus with your arms, is a good defense against this kind of attack.

However, from a personal philosophical perspective, the fly-in-the-ointment, so to speak, on psychic protection is that ultimately it is a counterproductive practice. In effect it is a "pushing away" or a rejection of reality. Such shelter is a way to avoid accepting the facts of how things actually are. We live in an imperfect and unpredictable world, and we are subject to all the vicissitudes that life can throw at us. Nature, despite the attitudes and attempts of governments and multinational corporations, is not under our control, nor do we have the ability to protect ourselves from the natural movements of the Earth. Maybe we can mitigate the impact of natural disasters to some extent, but we do not have the capabilities to absolutely safeguard human existence. We need no reminding of the immeasurable and endless amount of human suffering and destruction caused by war. We, as individuals and as a collective, are eminently vulnerable, and that we need to accept. Anybody who has been in a serious accident knows very well how frail the human body is.

Adverse conditions, setbacks, and upheavals happen in our personal lives. We can neither shape nor construct our personal world to conform to the notion of how things should be. If we followed the path of the soul warrior, we would stay present in our difficulty; we would not try to shelter from or avoid experiences that we regard as negative or emotionally challenging. We would open our inner stone fortress that has been our protection, stay with the diminishing feelings of powerlessness, our broken hearts, and allow ourselves to experience the pain and sorrow so that we could transcend and release those feelings, move to a state of inner peace, and awaken our compassion.

We develop our spiritual and emotional qualities when we are open to being present in the face of negative circumstances and people rather than avoiding them. This is the challenge faced by the soul warrior on his or her path to personal power, which requires transcending the limitations of the defended ego.

## THE SOUL WARRIOR

A soul warrior is any man or woman who has come to the realization that the conflict between heart and mind, between happiness and misery, lies within. Soul warriors do not project their inner turmoil onto the outer world or onto others. They know that it is from our dreams, our conscious or unconscious beliefs, that we create the world "out there." Many of us linguistically associate the term *warrior* with fighting or a soldier in battles and wars. For a shaman, the term has a totally different meaning.

Warriors are fully engaged with life and give their 100 percent maximum best, and then if they do not succeed, they are at peace with this outcome; they have done their best. They neither delude nor betray themselves with half-hearted actions or choices.

Warriors are at peace with ambiguity; they know that clarity is the enemy of wisdom and that confusion is a higher form of consciousness, a place where change must happen.

Warriors have learned never to judge another, as they know this says more about the warrior than about the one who is being judged.

Warriors knows that there is no such thing as an objective sacred. Either everything is sacred or nothing is sacred.

Warriors are ultimately creators, not destroyers.

Warriors accept responsibility for their actions and do not blame others for failure.

Warriors know that all of life is a rite of passage.

Warriors know that if they have to say they are warriors, then they are not.

Warriors do not ask, "Who am I?" They know that this is completely irrelevant. The question they may ask is "Where am I?"

The Dalai Lama remains an ever-present inspirational force in my life and an embodiment of the qualities of forgiveness, compassion, and peace. He is in effect a true soul warrior. At the end of a talk he gave in Los Angeles a few years ago, someone from the audience asked him, "Why didn't you fight back against the Chinese?"

The Dalai Lama looked down, swung his feet just a bit, then looked back up at us and said with a gentle smile, "Well, war is obsolete you know." Then, after a few moments, his face grave, he said, "Of course the mind can rationalize fighting back . . . but the heart, the heart would never understand. Then you would be divided in yourself, the heart and the mind, and the war would be inside you."

We hear or read of anecdotal stories in which people "feel" the presence of another person with them, or for some reason become obsessed with someone, or are unable to shake off the feeling of being watched or pursued. Some of you may have also had such experiences, and it is difficult to share them with friends or family for fear of ridicule or of having your feelings dismissed.

These situations are perceivable within the human energy body. In my experience, two reasons may be the cause.

When someone's emotions, such as anger, have been suppressed, these feelings are not expressed but are still present. The person may be unwilling or unable to cope with the pain or grief, or may harbor anger, hurt, and resentment for a husband, wife, parent, or partner. Intense, passionate, unexpressed emotions from the human energy field detach and can take on a life of their own. The frequency of this subfield resonates with a similar frequency, and this generates the link to another's field. When this occurs a person can sense a presence around him or her.

This autonomous subfield can have a malignant influence on people, and although they may not be consciously aware of it, it may leak out in some way. You may know people who on the surface are amiable but on occasion and *seemingly* out of character utter vicious, hurtful, and spiteful comments and act unpleasantly. Sometimes people's awareness becomes chronically detached from their dark feelings, and the autonomous subfield feels sinister and threatening. People may perceive this as an external entity, a psychic attack, or an evil spirit. When I see clients who have detached from their unacceptable feelings and experience themselves under pressure from this external force, it is critical to bring them into an awareness that they are sensing their own emotions. By going back to the source, that is, the event where this separation happened, they find the opportunity for acceptance, without self-judgment, and for eventual integration and healing.

From time to time I experience a variant of this, when people deny their inner darkness, or shadow, and adopt a spiritual persona as a way to evade their shadow. These "spiritual" individuals can make quite unpleasant comments, and when challenged, the fallback response is along the lines of "How could I do that? I have dedicated my entire life to the light." This is a sort of guru *disengagement* strategy. Do you know anyone like this?

Back in the days before the World Wide Web, I used to read old-fashioned newsletters printed on paper delivered in the mail. In such a newsletter from an organization of lightworkers, the first page was about their aspirations to spread light, love, and compassion on Earth as a spiritual sacred mission. However, on the second page, their virtuous tone dramatically changed as they ripped into, admonished, and ferociously castigated a different organization of lightworkers for the offense . . . wait for it . . . "of using the wrong type of light"!

To quote Jung on the concept of the shadow: "Filling the conscious mind with ideal conceptions is a characteristic of Western theosophy, but not the confrontation with the shadow and the world of darkness. One does not become enlightened by imagining figures of light, but by making the darkness conscious."[1]

I know it's a silly idea and will never take off and fly, but maybe for the fun of it we should turn the notion around and consider calling those striving to reach an enlightened state of consciousness not light-workers, but darkworkers.

## PLAYING WITH MULTIDIMENSIONAL REALITY CONSCIOUSNESS

Back in the 1970s I found the science fiction/fantasy series by Roger Zelazny inspirational. The novels revolved around the "one true realm," called Amber. It's a complex, intriguing, and exciting adventure story written over the course of eight or so books. Anyway, deep beneath Amber lies the "Pattern." Walking the Pattern allows the characters in effect to "create" or "shift" into alternate multidimensional reality by manipulating "shadow" stuff. This was achieved either by creating or transforming the reality of a character, bit by bit, element by element, a leaf here, a rock there, a path in another location, and so on until the place that the character wanted to go was *reached,* or *created* (this aspect was intriguingly ambiguous). The desired destination was held firmly in the character's imagination. There were also the "Trump" cards, in which various locations and characters were pictured, and when one of the protagonists in the novel wanted to contact another person, he or she would take out the respective Trump card and focus until the image became animated and the receiving person was aware of the contact. Then, either a dialogue would start or, in some cases, the receiver would physically "bring in" the character to whatever place or reality the receiver had located, a kind of a shortcut.

In my youthful way I found this whole concept stimulating and exciting, so I started to play with this. While I was walking, I began to imagine reality shifting bit by bit, and subjectively my perception shifted too. In this state of consciousness, walking along a street with parked cars, it appeared that I was stationary and the parked cars were moving. It's similar to the phenomenon of sitting in a train at a station and then an adjacent train moves; there is that uncanny feeling that your train is moving even though it is motionless. Yes, it is an illusion on the one hand, but on the other hand it is a way to *see* the world in another way.

I also made and painted my own set of Trump cards and started to experiment and play with the concept. During these moments of consciously exercising my imagination, my mind felt as if it was being stretched and expanded, and my dreams were more colorful and vivid. I began to experiment with postcards, particularly postcards of exotic foreign lands. Working with photographs of real places held a power an order of magnitude higher than the fantasized pictures. I concentrated on the image on the card, and when I was able to hold the image in my mind, I was able to "step" into the scene, with surprising results. It really felt as if I was there; I could feel the heat of the sun, smell the flowers and the sea, hear sounds—even though I had no physical body. I stopped doing these experiments in long-distance seeing because of major life changes. This was years before my accident in the elevator, a kind of foreshadowing of remote viewing technology.

Pablo Amaringo often emphasized the importance of perceiving the world in different ways. During our work together on the book he said:

The spirits teach that in order to cultivate our mind, we need to develop our perception; that is, to see things from a different perspective. If we look at an object from another viewpoint we gain a broader understanding. We can look at something both upside down and the right way up. You must read words differently; this enables both sides of your mind to work. For example, let's read this note here: [He is referring to my working papers on the table.] It says, "Inventory of Paintings." But looking at it the other way around it says, "Paintings of Inventory," which has another meaning. One then has another perspective. This is how you should read, both ways.[2]

## EXERCISE

### ✳ Developing Expanded Perception

1. Select a postcard of places that interest you, either geographically or historically, such as ancient temple ruins, the pyramids, or a picturesque bay. The suggested length for an initial journey is ten minutes. Later, after you're comfortable with journeying, extend the length to twenty or thirty minutes.

2. Find a quiet place where you will not be disturbed or distracted, and turn off the phone. Breathe in a relaxed and rhythmic pattern for a few minutes, and then, when you have a sense of being ready, study the image on the postcard. After a minute, close your eyes and see if you can hold the picture in your imagination. If not, resume studying the picture, and repeat the process until you feel that you can hold the image.

3. With your eyes closed and still holding the image in your mind, allow the picture to become three-dimensional. In other words, experience this as depth within the picture. As this happens you may feel a perceptible "click" or an energetic surge within your mind. Don't be alarmed if this occurs; this is an encouraging signal that your awareness is expanding.

4. When a perception of depth occurs, move into the picture. If you feel that you are making this up, it doesn't matter; continue to enter the scene, and tell yourself that you are there. Once a sense of being there is in place, start to navigate through the scene. Look behind the facade of buildings; see what is there. Do not negate or diminish any impressions or senses that you may have. Keep moving slowly, looking around. What can you hear? What can you smell? What feelings are being generated by this experience? Are there any unexpected scenes or occurrences that you feel you have not made up; for instance, do you have a sense of surprise at what is happening?

5. Whenever you are ready to conclude the exploration, turn around and retrace your steps until you are back at the place you started from. Become aware of your physical body, and gently release the image and scene from your mind. Take a few minutes to become fully aware of your physical body and surroundings. Jot some notes in your journal about this experience. Include your feelings and all sensory information.

6. When you have completed your journey, take a drink of tea, water, or juice, and reflect on the experience. Do you feel energized? Does your mind seem clearer? Do you feel sleepy and dreamy? If you answer the last question with "yes," take a moment for a short nap because this will help to integrate the experience.

The natural question to ask at this stage is: Was this all a fantasy or daydream, or was this authentic? The answer is that you don't know; the only way to validate the experience is to somehow get verification. Ways to gain validation include working with a postcard of a destination that you have not been to, yet are planning to visit, and looking for a scene from your journey once you get there, or you could ask a friend who has been to the destination to verify any part of your experience. You may be very surprised at the feedback.

One of the implicit and explicit threads woven through this and the previous chapters is an exploration of the human energy field, which is in itself an expression or manifestation of a greater universal field. The crux is how awareness of these fields can empower our individual and collective experience. In the following chapter we continue this exploration as we take a look at this universal field of energy and experientially discover ways we can utilize this "energy medicine" for the benefit of ourselves and others.

# 9

# THE COLORS OF INFINITY
## Becoming Cognizant of Bioenergy Fields

*There will come a time when a diseased condition will not be described as it is today by the physicians and psychologists, but it will be spoken of in musical terms, as one would speak of a piano that was out of tune.*

RUDOLF STEINER

Following the cosmological singularity of the big bang, the subatomic particles (energy) formed hydrogen, the most basic and profuse element (matter) in the universe. The hydrogen coalesced into stars as a result of gravitational forces. All the other elements were created from the eventual explosion of the stars. These elements combined, creating new and increasingly complex elements, such as carbon, which formed the fundamental constituent of biological life. We are the product of energy manifested as matter, and humanity is a part of the evolution of the universe. This is not a metaphor.

Two concepts at the heart of increasingly popular holistic healing methods are that the mind, body, and spirit are connected and that the body is a projection of an energetic field, or template. This is not exactly groundbreaking news or even New Age; shamans have understood these concepts for thousands of years. This holistic perspective is not shared to any degree by modern medicine, a reductionist system that establishes distinct specializations and discrete functionality.

The mind-body-spirit connection basically states that the body is not a machine assembled of individual components. Anything that affects a person at any level also affects the total person. The holistic approach takes into account all the factors in the treatment of illness and maintenance of well-being. In shamanism, the fundamental principle is that our field of energy determines our health and well-being. This bioenergy field* is strongly influenced by our mental state and emotions because they are part of the complex geometric pattern of this field. When we experience anguish, distress, or suffering, or enter into a negative and downward spiral of thinking in our lives, it manifests in our energy body as dissonance, discordant vibrations in the patterns of the field, which will eventually manifest in the physical body as illness, disease, or dysfunction. There is also an external factor; invasive forms of energy in our field are another major cause of illness. This is the why shamans heal the physical body through the energy field. This body of practices is known as shamanic extraction healing.

This intrusive energy scenario is not in any way a fanciful notion. We feel it in our physical body, and we use linguistic metaphors to describe it. We can feel "stabbed in the back," "chilled to the bone," "a pain in the neck," or that "something is eating away at me." We instinctively know when people hold a grievance or have an indignant feeling that the world has wronged them; these people have "a chip on their shoulder." It is not just an idiom; it can be sensed as a presence or felt as a weight on their shoulder. An underlying energy accompanies

---

*Scientific research into bioenergetic phenomena is increasing. The human body emits light particles called *biophotons,* or *ultraweak photon emissions.* They are part of the electromagnetic spectrum (380–780 nanometers) and can be measured by modern instruments.

stinging, stabbing comments from others. This is an intrusive, penetrating energy, creating dissonance in our field. If this energy is allowed to flow and release, all is well and good. If it is blocked or repressed, then we can feel unwell, and later, physical symptoms can occur.

From the shamanic perspective, we all have an energy body, although in the West this concept is neither accepted nor understood. When people are angry or envious, or have a pervasive bad attitude, they direct not just verbal harshness but also antagonistic energy to others without realizing they are doing it, thereby inflicting harm. If you are aware and working to achieve a higher consciousness, it is vital that you cultivate the quality of self-discipline. I am not suggesting that you shouldn't be angry with someone—that is nonsense and a denial of your humanity and honest emotions—but you need to control the raw energy of anger and not direct it at another. Develop techniques that allow you to safely dissipate or transform this energy. Forgiveness for yourself and the other party is a powerful way to release this discordant energy. I related in the first chapter that I had a massive chip on my shoulder; I was filled with resentment for the screw-up that caused my accident in the elevator. It was only when I gritted my teeth and with all my heart forgave the people who caused the accident through their carelessness that my life changed and the way to healing and new adventures started.

Homeopathy is one of the longstanding holistic healing methods that embody the concept that the human energy body is the causal template for physical health. Homeopathy is based on the principle of "like cures like," so symptoms are treated with a highly diluted dose of the applicable compound. The dose is so highly diluted that eventually there may not even be a discernable physical trace of the original compound remaining in the medicine. The medicine contains the energy pattern of the original substance, and it is this energy that influences the human energy body to resolve the dissonant pattern. This in turn enables the body's innate healing faculties to clear the physical symptoms.

I am very enthusiastic about the efficaciousness of homeopathy, and I believe that energy medicine such as this is the medicine of the future. Over ten years ago when I became ill, I went to see my doctor, whose eyes grew wide when I showed him the problem. He said that it could be a serious problem and that it was urgent to get tests at the hospital. Instinctively, I was unsure that it would be a good idea to go down that route, so I contacted a friend, Lorraine Grayston, who is an outstanding homeopath. The following day she came by with another friend, Dawn Russel, who was studying with her. They asked me a range of questions about this illness, and each round of questions became increasingly focused. One of the last questions was "Have you been eating more oranges than usual?" This question really grabbed my attention. Although I did not usually eat oranges, I had recently started to drink about three liters of orange juice a day. When all the questions were completed, I received the medicine. In three days the physical symptoms and the fever had completely vanished, and I was fully fit again. I know firsthand that homeopathy works.

## EXERCISE

### ✳ Perceiving Natural Energy Fields

There are a number of ways to perceive the energy field.

1. To begin this interesting exploration, rub your hands together for a minute. This rubbing stimulates the energy field. Then place your hands in front of you with the fingertips a few millimeters apart over a dark background. Gently look at the spaces between the fingertips, and you will start to see a milky wisp flowing in the spaces. This is your bioenergy field. Focus on this while moving your fingertips very slowly apart, and you will see the field expand to fill the space. Once you perceive this, close the gap slowly, and then again gently move the fingertips apart. Repeat this cycle a few times and then you will feel the "magnetic" attraction between the fingertips. Maintaining your attention while carrying out this exercise will stimulate your energy

field. You may also have a sense of this, very much like a tingling around your body.

2. Place your hand, palm facing downward, just above the underside of your bare arm to avoid touching the hair. (The underside of your arm should be facing up.) Move your hand very slowly along your arm, and then slowly back. Repeating this a few times stimulates the energy field. Once you feel a tingling or heat emanating from your hand, look at your arm against a dark background, and you should perceive your energy field. The more you do this, the easier and clearer it becomes. You can also practice this with a friend.

3. Try this with plants: Place the palm of your hand just above a leaf, and direct a warm feeling toward the plant. This stimulates the plant's energy field. Gently move your hand above the surface and edges of the leaf against a dark background. You may feel a tingling sensation in your hand as you do this. It is easier to carry out this exercise with fast-growing plants such as tomato or mint.

We can open up and expand the ability to perceive energy by seeing in a different way. In effect we return to seeing the world like we did when we were children. Unfortunately, due to the everyday hustle and bustle of our lives, many of us have become sensory indifferent, or even fatigued. It is if we have lost our passion with the world and have severed the magical connection we once had. However, when we were young, everything that we saw, heard, or felt was a totally new sensory experience. If you have watched a young child look at something new, you will understand this.

You can expand your sensory perception further by simply looking at things in a different way. Play with this like it is a game. For example, go out for a walk and look at a tree that you have looked at previously, and instead of just seeing the form of the tree, observe the spaces between the branches and the leaves; alter your view as if you were seeing the tree for the very first time. Look at familiar things in your house this way, or turn things upside down. When you look at photographs or paintings, take in the small details, the shapes between the forms. Get a different perspective. Change the way that you see things. A friend of mine, the artist Slocum Hewson, told me that when he teaches people to draw an object he gets them to turn the object upside down, and people who are convinced they cannot draw find themselves drawing the object perfectly. It is this deconstruction of and eventual disengagement from a preconceived paradigm that liberates energy, erases set boundaries, and liberates dormant creative power.

Another method is to develop an idiosyncratic, abstract view. Normally we see from our subjective perspective, our individual frame of reference. It is our naturally evolved cognitive way since the beginning of our species. Taking an alternative visual perspective does not happen of its own accord; it needs to be practiced. To do this we turn our point of view around in our imagination and project it on the object itself. So, for example, instead of seeing an apple fall off a tree, turn it around and see it from the viewpoint of the apple. Maybe you perceive that from the apple's perspective, it appears that the ground is rushing up toward it. You can also adjust the scale and go microscopic. Imagine a bee landing on a flower. How does it appear from the bee's perspective? How does it appear from the flower's aspect? Although it is a quirky notion, we often do this kind of "view changing" looking out of an airplane window, watching the landscape from the viewpoint of a bird.

These are fun things to do, and, more important, it is a useful practice to expand your sensory perception; it is a way to see the world in a new way, just like a child.

If you want to experience the difference between natural bioenergy fields and human-made, or mechanical, energy fields, place the palm of your hand above the cable of a domestic device that has been turned on. Here the difference is very noticeable; the natural field has a subtle flowing quality, while the device has a relentless, unvarying pulsation, a mechanical characteristic.

Practicing sensing energy fields is the first step to working with shamanic extraction methods. Extraction is a traditional way to address invasive and misplaced forms of energy, the precursors of physical illness in the human energy field.

Working with natural objects augments the shamanic extraction practice. I often use feathers and stones. A feather is a precision instrument in detecting anomalies and dissonance in a person's energy field. However, these natural objects are not just "tools": there is an ineffable spiritual aspect to them. I learned from the Amazonian shamans in the practice known as the diet that a natural object is not a separate thing that you use as a tool. It possesses spirit, so to work with natural objects, it is important that you have a positive attitude and good feelings toward them. You have to enter into a partnership with them. If you do this, you will find that they will work in conjunction with you and guide you.

First, you will need to obtain a feather. This is not always straightforward because the feathers you find on the ground are usually in poor condition unless there has been a recent molt. One suggestion is to get in touch with a bird sanctuary to ask about the possibility of acquiring a suitable feather. An exchange, such as a donation to the sanctuary, is an equitable action. I have found that the flight feathers, or remiges, of raptor birds such as owls, buzzards, hawks, eagles, and condors are suitable for this (see color plate 3).

*Important note:* In the United States it is illegal to possess (under any circumstances) raptor feathers without a special permit from the U.S. Fish and Wildlife Service. As an alternative, turkey feathers have a firm edge to work with, and it is not illegal to possess them. In the United Kingdom it is permitted to own feathers of wild birds if you have proof that you have lawfully obtained them. I strongly recommend that you verify the regulations and laws in the country or region where you live to make sure that owning feathers is not an offense.

When traveling, be circumspect about the selling techniques used by local people to encourage you to buy artifacts such as feathers. On a recent group trip to Peru, I cautioned everyone about this, with particular emphasis on buying feathers. The following day, one of my friends in the group proudly showed us the condor feather he had just purchased. He said that it was okay and pointed out a white line on the edge of the feather. The man who had sold him the feather informed him that the white line indicated that the feather had fallen off naturally. I smiled at this and said, "He would have told you anything, even that the bird had alighted in front of him, plucked the feather out with its beak, and presented it to him on a silver platter." My friend got the message and realized that buying feathers only encourages the hunting of these magnificent birds.

## EXERCISE

### ✳ Removing Blockages from the Energy Field

You will need the assistance of a friend, who will pretend to be the client. The client lies down on the ground while you scan his or her energy field.

1. Very slowly move the feather approximately eight to ten inches above your friend's body. Start at the head and scan down to the feet. Place your maximum attention on the feather's edge as you carefully move it along. As you do this, you may perceive the bioenergy field in distinct ways. For instance, the edge of the feather could vibrate when it moves to a position above the blockage. You could also receive an image of the nature of the blockage in your "mind's eye" or have a different sensory feeling.

2. Observe the movements of the feather. At times it may suddenly rise or drop. Make a mental note of the locations in which those movements occur. Complete the circuit of moving the feather along, noting other "blocked" or "stagnant" areas. Then talk to your friend about the results of the initial scan and get some feedback. Did the blocked or stagnant

locations or the locations where the feather made a noticeable vertical movement resonate with the client? Was there a correlation between the areas with the most movement and the client's sense of stagnation or blockage? In all likelihood you will be told that there is a problem where you noticed movement in the feather, maybe soreness, pain, or swelling.

3. Once you have established the main area to focus on, start at the head, slowly move the feather to the target area, and direct your attention there. Close your eyes, and allow your inner vision to inform you. Let whatever impressions come to you percolate and take shape. Then slowly lower the feather and let it glide along and around the area. Soon you may have identified the shape of the dissonance; it may be a depression, a protuberance, or simply a flat area that seems strange.

4. Trusting your intuition, begin to release the blocked area. As you place your attention on the blockage, sense that its tactile texture becomes gradually less hard and increasingly softer and more malleable. Continue this until the block has dissipated and the energy feels consistent with unblocked areas. Again, discuss this with your friend, share your experience, and get feedback. How is your friend feeling? Is there a difference?

Take a short break, and then continue working with your client, or swap roles.

It is also possible to directly extract physical intrusions (not energy intrusions) without physical contact using a feather. On a shamanic healing practitioner's course some years ago, a participant hobbled into the hall. She said that in the previous week, a large thorn had got buried in the sole of her foot. It was fortuitous that this was the shamanic extraction module and that I had my feather box with me. With the group witnessing this "demonstration," I examined her foot and found that the thorn had penetrated deep inside and was not visible. I worked with the owl feather and sensed the intrusion. In my mind I moved the edge of the feather underneath the thorn and started to slowly lift it up. It took about thirty minutes and required intense concentration.

Eventually, a dark spot appeared on her foot. As I continued to lift the intrusion, the thorn began to emerge, and when it stuck out sufficiently, I used tweezers to gently extract it. The thorn was more than an inch in length and curved like a hook. Here the feather was a conduit for the spirit healers. This happens when you establish a partnership with the nonphysical aspect of the feather. At times you can perceive or feel the spirit of the bird assisting you in this work.

## THE POWER OF STONES

Stones have power. From a shamanic perspective they are alive and a gift from the mineral kingdom. Minerals are the foundation of all life, and without them, plant, animal, and human existence would not be possible. The esoteric and religious use of stones spans the millennia. Stones that are venerated for religious worship or are at the centerpiece of sacred sites are known as a *baetyli*. In Western culture, for example, in the myth "The Sword in the Stone," the magical sword Excalibur is embedded in a stone, and only the rightful king could withdraw it. For centuries, the Stone of Scone, also known as the Stone of Destiny, was placed under the royal throne for the coronation of the new British monarch. The London Stone is also the stuff of legend: "So long as the Stone of Brutus is safe, so long shall London flourish," as the old saying goes. Brutus was the mythological founder of London, and the London Stone is regarded as the foundation stone of London.

One of the most magical stories from the Old Testament, in Genesis 28, tells how Jacob escapes from his brother, Esau, and at night falls asleep on a stone. This stone pillow is where he has his famed dream of the ladder with angels ascending and descending, and standing at the pinnacle is God. When Jacob awakens, he anoints the stone with oil and names the stone Bethel, meaning "House of El" or "House of God." This archetypal baetylus later became the most important religious center in biblical Israel until Solomon built the Temple in Jerusalem.

Another acclaimed baetylus is the sacred stone known as the *omphalos,* located in the Temple of Apollo at Delphi. Omphalos means "navel," and it was regarded as the center, or navel, of the world. Interestingly, in the Quechua language of the Andes, the name of the ancient Inca city Cuzco also means "navel of the world." Ancient philosophers understood that the navel is our first conduit of nourishment and is associated with life itself and that the term *navel of the world* was deeply symbolic. Furthermore, in sacred geometry, the navel represents the golden ratio, or phi ($\phi$). The sacred stones from many mythologies symbolize the axis mundi.

In the vibrant mythological and shamanic *mundo Amazónica,** stones possess mysterious and potent energy. Pablo Amaringo describes *encantos,* the magical stones used by shamans for healing (see color plate 4): "Encantos possess hidden powers that can be combined with *ícaros* [magical chants sung by shamans] to heal." Pablo cautions that one should be careful when encountering encantos in an ayahuasca vision, because "their esoteric powers cannot be received by a person who has not first dieted and purged with ayahuasca. Some encantos are so powerful that if they are seen by a person who has not dieted properly, they can cause *daño* [harm]."[1]

For a shaman, one of the most important properties of stones and gemstones is that they "hold" energy. In Peru, stones endowed with energy are shaped into talismans, amulets, and charms to attract love. These are called *huacanqui.* Other stones are used to protect a person from negativity, such as hostility and envy; these are known as a *seguro,* Spanish for "safe" or "secure."

---

*A term used by Pablo Amaringo to describe the world of the Amazon rainforest.

EXERCISE

## ✳ Discovering the Power of Stones

1. Start by establishing an affinity with the stone. This is not so enigmatic as it appears because all actions start with an intent. An intention is an act of power. The principle of intention functions on two levels: The first level is deciding "this is what I want to do; this is where I want to go." The second level is the antecedent, a signal or alert for energy to move to a certain destination or objective.

2. Once you have made a clear intention to find the stone, the primary act is to choose a stone or allow one to choose you. The stone in some way will draw your attention to it. The stone can be anywhere—on a beach, by the side of the road, or even in the parking lot of a pub (where I have found some of my best stones). Do not judge the stone by its appearance or the location where you find it. Pick up the stone and, while holding it, get a sense of it. Does it feel right? Does it feel as if the stone wants to be with you? Trust your feelings on this.

3. When you have some time, look carefully at the stone, study its details, observe its facets, and get to know it. Meditate on whether there is a particular quality that you need to bring into your life, such as love, courage, trust, confidence, creativity, or serenity.

4. Next, plan a shamanic journey to find the particular quality that you need. Place the stone in your hand, and start the journey. You will mostly likely find that this quality is embodied in an object or an artifact that you are magnetically drawn to in the journey. Once you find this artifact and either instinctively know that it is the correct item or are informed of this by your spirit guide, hold it in your hands and start your return to everyday consciousness. As you make the transition to the here and now, you will feel the energy of the artifact in your hands. Once you have returned, cup your hands and forcefully blow the energy into the stone. Feel, sense, and imagine that the quality is moving into the stone itself. You can often sense the stone pulsating in your hands as you do this.

5. The next step is to diet the stone. Although dieting usually takes place in the context of plants, Pablo Amaringo told me this method is also used for communion with *encantos*, or magical stones. In this diet, the consciousness of the shaman and the stone meet to establish a magical affinity.

   To diet the stone, place it in a jug of water, cover it, and keep the jug in a cool and dry place for eight days. Starting on the ninth day, slowly drink a half glass of the water each morning until the water is gone. As you sip the "charged" water, use your imagination and feel that you are ingesting the quality that you brought back from the shamanic journey. This practice can also be used with gemstones and crystals.

6. After this, keep the stone with you, place it on your altar, or put it under your pillow at night. Go with what feels right for you; this is a personal interaction between you and the stone. There is nothing whimsical about this; it imbues the stone with a sacred quality that is keyed to you. In other words, it is a personal baetylus in your life.

## USING HERBS AND RESINS

A fascinating and helpful way to sense energy fields is with the smoke from herbs, wood, or tree resins. The origin of this technique is in *smudging,* a shamanic practice used to clear negative or "out of place" energy using the smoke from bundles of dried herbs, typically sage, lavender, or rosemary. In the Amazon the delightfully aromatic tree called *palo santo,* literally "holy stick," is used for this purpose. Additionally, the locally grown tobacco *Nicotiana rustica,* known in South America as *mapacho,* is one of the most important plants used by shamans in the Amazon for cleansing and purification. This tobacco is usually smoked in shredded form (rolled as a cigarette, which is also called a mapacho, or in a *cashimbo,* a carved wood pipe). Or it is smoked in a *puro* (a "cigar" made of rolled leaves). The smoke from copal, a tree resin, is also used.

Using smoke to sense energy fields is similar to working with a feather, as described earlier. The key is to gently direct the smoke toward a person. Start from a distance of about twelve inches, and gently fan the smoke around the person. Place maximum attention on the smoke, and see what happens. Does the smoke hesitate and then shy away or does it recoil before it reaches the person's body? Is the smoke pulled in as if by a vortex? Note these reactions, and when you have completed the practice discuss your findings with the person as per the exercise with the feathers.

I discussed linguistic metaphors for intrusive energy earlier, and those apply here as well. If a person feels "stabbed in the back" or has a "chip on his shoulder," the smoke will generally reveal this by recoiling from those areas.

## THE ENERGY OF THE MIND

Let's turn now to the concept that thoughts are energy, which has been an underlying idea throughout this book. From a shamanic point of view, *thought* is not an abstract notion but is in fact a perceptible energy. At times during an ayahuasca ceremony, I can see the "thought field"; it appears to me as a vast geometric, three-dimensional, interlaced, luminous net. Each node on this mesh is a spherical cluster with antenna connecting it with other nodes. The visionary artist Alex Grey depicts this geometric structure in many of his amazing paintings.

This is a fundamental concept for a variety of spiritual, personal-development, and shamanic practices. Positive thinking, the law of affirmation, and the law of attraction operate on the basis that thoughts attract experiences that we wish for or think about, for better or worse. If we are in a negative, downward spiral of thinking, then we attract the experiences that we fear and want to avoid. This also relates to the notion that we create our own reality, and to a certain extent that is valid. However, there are far larger forces, such as nature and the Earth, that form the preeminent reality of our lives. It is a magnificent piece of spiritual hubris to believe that we create our reality. I prefer the viewpoint that we *co-create* our reality. Looking at it this way, you might say, "What brought me to a volcano that is about to explode?" rather than "Why did I cause the volcano to explode?"

One of my favorite stories from the Carlos Castaneda books tells how Carlos reads a newspaper with a headline screaming about the increasing level of muggings in Mexico City. He asks his teacher, Don Juan, what he could do if he was in the city and attacked by muggers. Would he run or would he fight? Don Juan starts laughing, and he laughs and laughs. In fact, he laughs so much that he ends up rolling around on the ground gripped by this laughter. When Don Juan recovers, gets it back together, and can finally speak, he informs his totally bewildered apprentice that he would simply not be there!

This anecdote attests to an important principle: from a mind perspective, we reap what we sow. Therefore, it is important to be aware of our discordant and antagonistic thoughts, as they will co-create our reality. It is nothing new; many people experience this kind of discordance and the inevitable manner in which it ripples throughout the day. The idiom "getting out of the wrong side of the bed" is an apt metaphor for our energy manifesting in the world. We wake up grumpy and surly, which results in a day filled with frustration and aggravation. It's one of those days that you wish you had just gone back to bed.

The "thoughts are energy" concept underlies the enigmatic power of the *placebo effect,* in which a patient is given a fake medicine that for all intents and purposes has the look and feel of the actual medicine. If the patient thinks that it will be helpful, then to the dismay of the pharmaceutical companies, this inert product often is. The placebo effect is a real and measurable phenomenon, and it illustrates how our thoughts and beliefs affect our body. The opposite of this is the notorious nocebo effect, discussed previously, in which a doctor's diagnosis of a serious disease can have a dramatic effect. When a doctor's negative attitude and outlook are transmitted to the patient, they afflict the patient's thoughts and beliefs, creating emotional trauma in the form of discouragement, depression, and despondency. This is the antithesis of healing and invariably makes a critical situation worse. In olden days, a nocebo would be called a curse, which effectively it is.

## THE SHAPE OF SOUND

Pablo Amaringo describes in his art how shamans use colors, shapes, and sounds, which are all symmetrical patterns of energy. He says, "All movement creates a vibration or sound; even the movement of nonphysical matter has a vibration, an ultrasound that underlies the harmonic structure of physical matter. You can sometimes visually perceive this when in the ayahuasca *mareación* [visionary trance state]; color and sound are the same and you realize that both are the vibration of matter."[2]

*Synesthesia* is the term used for a sensory experience in which there is a "crossover," or union, between the senses. Sounds and shapes can have an aroma, for instance, or a color. People who have synesthesia perceive the world in a very different way than the majority. For some reason it is regarded as a neurocognitive disorder. In my view, it is an evolutionary ontogenesis toward an expanded multisensory experience.

I have experienced this union of the senses with entheogens such as ayahuasca and San Pedro (*Echinopsis pachanoi*), a cactus native to the Andes. The sounds of the shaman's *shacapa* (leaf-bundle rattle) and *maraca* (seed-filled gourd) generate visible colors and patterns—a wonderful sensory experience. At times during an ayahuasca ceremony, when I have been chanting the ícaros (chants learned directly from plants that are sung by shamans during ayahuasca ceremonies), the experience becomes magical. As I am chanting, the sounds form visible geometric patterns, and the patterns form into shapes, creating a visual soundscape. The energy patterns of people are perceptible, and where there is a dissonance in their field, the patterns of the ícaros create a harmony that has a tangible and balancing effect.

Traditional cultures understand that sound is, in effect, audible energy. This is the underlying concept of the art of the Shipibo people of the Upper Amazon, which depicts highly complex geometric patterns (see color plate 5). These patterns represent an all-pervading magical reality that can challenge the Western linguistic heritage and rational mind.

These patterns are more than an expression of the oneness of creation, the interchangeability of light and sound, the union or fusion of perceived opposites; they depict an ongoing dialogue or communion with the spiritual world and the powers of the rainforest. The visionary art of the Shipibo brings this paradigm into a physical form. The ethnologist Angelika Gebhart-Sayer calls this "visual music."

The people of the Peruvian Amazon include a number of ethnic groups, each with its own language, traditions, and culture. The Shipibo, one of the largest ethnic groups, currently number about twenty thousand and inhabit communities throughout the Ucayali River region. They are highly regarded in the Amazon as masters of ayahuasca.

All the textile painting, embroidery, and artisan crafts are carried out by the women (see color plate 6). From a young age the Shipiba (Shipibo females) are initiated by their mothers and grandmothers into this practice. Teresa Rango, a Shipiba friend who works with me on our Amazon retreats, told me, "When I was a young girl, my mother squeezed drops of the *piripiri* [a species of *Cyperus*] berries into my eyes so that I would have the vision for the designs; this is only done once and lasts a lifetime."[3]

The intricate Shipibo designs have their origin in the nonmanifest and ineffable spirit world of the rainforest. The designs are representative of the Cosmic Serpent, or Great Mother, an anaconda called Ronin that created the universe (see color plate 7). For the Shipibo the skin of Ronin is a radiating, electrifying vibration of light, color, sound, and movement and is the embodiment of all possible patterns and designs, past, present, and future. The designs that the Shipibo paint are channels or conduits for this multisensorial vibrational fusion of form, light, and sound. Although in our cultural paradigm we consider art to be bound within the border of the material used, to the Shipibo the patterns extend far beyond these borders and permeate the entire world.

In the Shipibo worldview, our state of health (which includes physical and psychological well-being) is dependent on the balance of mind, spirit, and body. If an imbalance occurs, such as through the emotions of envy, hate, or anger, this will generate a negative effect on the health of that person. The shaman reestablishes the balance by chanting the ícaros, the audio code of the geometric patterns of harmony. From the shamanic perspective, there is no difference between the visual and acoustic codes.

A key element in this magical dialogue with the energy that permeates creation and is embedded in the Shipibo designs is the work with ayahuasca by the Shipibo shamans. When the shamans are deep in an ayahuasca trance, the ayahuasca reveals the luminous geometric patterns of energy. These filaments transform into the ícaros. The vocal range of the Shipibo shamans is astonishing; their chants flow from the highest falsetto to a resonating bass sound, and then transform to a gentle, soothing, melodic lullaby. In my personal experience, I have felt that every cell in my body is floating and embraced in a nurturing, all-encompassing vibration, and even the air around me vibrates in acoustic resonance with the ícaro of the maestro. The shaman knows when the healing is complete because the design is clearly distinct in the patient's body. It can take a few sessions to complete this, and when completed the geometric healing designs are embedded in the patient's body. This is called an *arkana,* a field of protective energy (see color plate 8).

In the West, the research by Dr. Hans Jenny has dramatically revealed the spectacular geometric forms created by sound using sand on a vibrational plate. As the sound changes the sand immediately creates different geometric patterns and complex mandalas. Dr. Jenny named this phenomenon *cymatics,* the study of how sound affects physical matter. On YouTube, you can see videos showing how sound creates beautiful geometric patterns in sand particles and in liquids. These three-dimensional shapes are stunning (see color plate 9).

The hearing range for humans lies between 20 Hz (hertz) and 20 kHz (kilohertz), and as we get older, our hearing range decreases. (The hertz scale measures how many times a second a sound wave is generated.) Police in the United States and the United Kingdom are utilizing high-frequency sound to disperse gatherings of teenagers. The sound is like a disturbing high-pitched mosquito buzzing that is outside the hearing range of older people.

In comparison, dolphins have a hearing range up to 150 kHz. Recent research published by the Dolphin Institute[4] suggests that the high-frequency sounds that dolphins produce are a highly evolved form of sonar. The echoes reflected by an object are perceived by the dolphin as an image of the object.

Recent experiments using an anechoic chamber indicate that the vibrational energy of sound is essential for humans. The anechoic chamber was originally developed to measure the sound level of products, for example, automobiles and washing machines. It is built to sustain complete silence, and any sound that is made in the chamber is swallowed up by the acoustic environment. It is a bewildering experience for volunteers sitting in a chamber. Within thirty minutes, subjects become disoriented, find it difficult to maintain their physical balance, and start to hallucinate. So far the record for staying in an anechoic chamber is forty-five minutes.[5]

## LISTENING TO THE WORLD

Earlier I discussed seeing the world in a different way to expand sensory perception. We can also practice hearing the world in a new way. Although we do not take our hearing sense for granted, we tend to use it unconsciously as a passive receiver rather than actively, as with the visual sense. Make a mindful plan to develop conscious awareness of your hearing, such as in situations where you single out one voice in a group of people. Our cognition acts as a sieve in our everyday soundscape, so be aware when you filter out familiar background sounds. As an act of attention, listen carefully when people are talking. Sound is a vibration that your body receives, in addition to your ears, so "feel" the words you're listening to. You can feel when words have less substance or weight, and this allows you to discern the vibrational difference between bullshit and truth. Try this out when you listen to interviews with politicians.

# 10

# AYAHUASCA, ENTHEOGENS, AND SACRAMENTAL PLANTS

*There is a transcendental dimension beyond language. It's just hard as hell to talk about it.*

TERENCE MCKENNA

Interest in ayahuasca and plant entheogens has surged in the past three decades. It is part of the renaissance of expanded consciousness and new thinking that was kindled in the 1960s. This resurgence has brought together a novel way of perceiving the visible and invisible patterns composing our world. Thought-provoking books from pioneers of consciousness research, such as *The Tao of Physics,* by Fritjof Capra, and those of Terence McKenna and Timothy Leary, have not only drawn parallels between the spiritual teachings of the East and the concepts of modern physics but at their heart have accentuated a universal consciousness permeating all things.

There is little doubt that an intimate relationship between the human world and the plant world has existed for thousands of years. Entheogenic plants were crucial in the religious and spiritual development of humans, awakening us to the ecstatic spiritual experience. In Terence McKenna's book *Food of the Gods,* he postulates the involvement of entheogens in the evolution of human consciousness and in the accelerated development of the human brain. Entheogens provide a powerful route for directly experiencing the sacred. They enable us to seek out the meaning of being human and our place in the universe; they allow us to perceive the blessings of the world that surrounds us and that we help to form.

Without a doubt entheogens offer the potential to explore and transform human consciousness, allowing us to bring an inclusive spirituality to our society and to alleviate the alienation from nature that has brought humanity to a grave ecological crisis.

Entheogens are not recreational and are not suitable for everybody. Working with them requires a certain attitude, discipline, and mental stability. Some Westerners view entheogens as a universal panacea and might believe that one session with ayahuasca would solve all their problems. Although I cannot exclude that possibility, in my experience, it is unlikely.

Ayahuasca is a combination of two primary plants, although other plants may be added to elicit certain visionary or healing experiences. The first is the ayahuasca vine (*Banisteriopsis caapi*) and the second, chacruna leaf (*Psychotria viridis*); together, they operate in a specific manner to affect our neurochemistry. The leaf contains the neurotransmitters of the tryptamine family (identical to those present in our brain), and the vine acts as an inhibitor to prevent our body's enzymes from breaking the tryptamines down, thereby making them inert. Science defines these as monoamine oxidase inhibitors (MAOIs), and they form the basis for many of the antidepressant pharmaceutical medications, such as Prozac and Seroxat. The MAOI principle was discovered by Western science in the 1950s, yet interestingly it has been known by the plant shamans for thousands of years, and when you ask the shamans how they knew of it, the response is invariably "the plants told us."

I have discovered that ayahuasca is a medicine, and unlike the Western understanding of medicine, it works on every level—on our physical bodies, our consciousness, our emotions, and our spirit. It is as if you are not just drinking a liquid brew but imbibing an "other" intelligence that knows exactly what is needed to help you. This is a communion in the true sense of the word, an intense experience of euphoria and ecstasy. It takes you on a journey of deep and profoundly meaningful personal and transpersonal insights, turning a searchlight on hidden thoughts and feelings in the subconscious mind, allowing an erasure of the ego boundaries and a merging with the greater field of consciousness.

We humans have a special relationship with and dependence on plants. Since our beginnings, they have been the source, both directly and indirectly, of our food, our shelter, our medicines, our fuel, our clothing, and of course the very oxygen that we breathe. This is common knowledge, and in general we take it for granted. Yet in Western culture we view plants as semi-inanimate, lacking the animating force labeled soul, mind, or spirit. Many people ridicule and regard as eccentric those who say they communicate with plants.

The biggest challenge for a Westerner undertaking this communion with plants is to accept that a person can experience nonmaterial reality by seeking out plant consciousness, and to do this requires a significant leap of the imagination.

How can we enter into a communion (in the true sense of the word) with plant consciousness? This can indeed be difficult, as Western culture has long forgotten this body of knowledge. However, we can learn from those peoples who still live within the paradigm of human and plant communication. The body of practices known as the diet in Amazonian shamanism opens the door to this world.

The diet, as mentioned previously, is a complex and challenging discipline required of Amazonian shamans, who wish to learn directly from the plant spirits. It implies much more than the mere dietary restrictions of avoiding salt, sugar, meat, and alcohol. It also means refraining from libidinous thoughts and sexual activity. The diet should be carried out in isolation without any social activities or stimulation. This attenuation of our primal human instincts cultivates us to become more "plantlike," thereby incorporating the plant consciousness into our own, allowing us to access plants' knowledge. During this time of intense communion, shamans learn the ícaros to invoke the power of the plants and methods for using the plants for healing.

The power of plants can take many forms—the colors of the flowers, the perfume, the shape, and so on. Maestro Artidoro Aro Cardenas explains:

A smell has the power to attract. I can also make smells to attract business, people who buy. You just rub it on your face and it brings in the people to your business, if you are selling, people come to buy. I also make perfumes for love, and others for flourishing. These are the forces of nature, what I do is give it direction with my breath so it has effect. I use my experience of the plants which I have dieted. I have a relation with the plants and with the patient—I can't make these things on a commercial scale. When I diet I take in the strength of the plant and it stays with me. Later I find the illness or suffering of the person, or what it is they want, and the plant guides me and tells me if it is the right one for that person, and I cure them.[1]

In my quest for shamanic knowledge, I dieted some of the teacher plants such as *ajo sacha* (*Mansoa alliacea*). When I first reached communion with this plant, I felt my senses being altered, expanded in some ineffable way, and I became aware of the song, the very rhythm, of the rainforest. Sounds, smells, and sights surrounded me that I had not been aware of in my normal, everyday waking state. I have been dieting ajo sacha for years now and continue to experience the fascinating phenomenon of heightened senses. With this incredible plant I can zoom in to hear or amplify distant sounds in the rich rainforest panorama. I can also hear high-pitched sound that usually is out of my hearing range. It is like floating within a living, three-dimensional sensorial experience of sound, color, smell, movement, and vibration—all in harmony and great beauty. In this state of expanded awareness, I realized that the rainforest was one entity, with the insects, birds, and animals being a part of its totality. I tried to diet this plant back in England, but I had to stop because the everyday clamor of traffic and machines was too harsh and jarring.

The work with the visionary plants not only provides a philosophical frame of reference for my life but is a path for deep soul healing. It generates a desire to engage fully and enthusiastically with the world around me. Celestial visions are always very nice and pleasing, but they must never cloud, disguise, or distract our real purpose, which is to fully embody our humanity.

I'd like to share a personal anecdote to exemplify this idea. In the late 1990s I led a group to the Amazon rainforest. Our initial gathering to introduce ourselves took place in the presence of our shaman, Javier Arevalo. Javier was very curious about Westerners and was interested in knowing what we were searching for with the visionary plants. One participant stood up and said she wanted a clear and definitive understanding of the male and female principles of the universe, the cosmic "yin and yang," as she literally put it. Well, Javier was totally mystified by this question; when I have attended his sessions with local people who visit him for a consultation, they ask about everyday problems and concerns, such as "Is my boyfriend (or husband, or girlfriend) cheating on me?" or "Why am I unlucky in finding a job?" We worked with the participant to explore the real question behind her initial enquiry, and finally she said that she was really looking for love in her life. Of course, Javier could understand this deep desire completely and was subsequently able to help her discover and reconcile the inner obstacles that had been preventing this.[2]

The teacher plants can provide a doorway to great and meaningful insights in the adventure of personal growth and healing. This allows us to access our higher order consciousness, a flowing, omnipresent force guiding our life. Among the many gifts that I have received from ayahuasca are unexpected insights into the world, humanity, what makes us what we are, why we do what we do, with all the permutations of these concerns.

In one experience in 2001 (an interesting synchronicity), while in the Amazon, I drank the brew and moved into a deep reverie. It felt as if everything around and within me was moving simultaneously, as if I had become part of a spiraling vortex of consciousness. I beamed into what I felt to be the center of creation. I was in the cosmos witnessing its totality: the formation of planets, stars, nebulas, and entire universes. Intricate geometric patterns stretched as far as the eye could see, changing size and form with fluid complexity. The chanting of the shaman filled every cell with an electric force, and every part of my body vibrated. It felt as if I was bodily lifted into the air, where I existed within a temple of sound, vibration, and bliss. Gathered around me were giants in ornate costumes of gold and multicolored feathers blowing smoke and fanning me. These were the spirits of ayahuasca.

I was no longer in my body, and my mind was set free to roam. Then a magnetic force drew me into Stanley Kubrick's masterpiece, *2001: A Space Odyssey*. I was not just observing but present three-dimensionally in the opening scene, the prologue entitled "The Dawn of Man," set millions of years in the past. I knew it was a movie, but it felt totally real. In this scene a group of hominids face extinction because the only water hole has been taken over by a different group of hominids. I watched as one of the disenfranchised group sees the black monolith that has materialized, and then in some form of telepathic transmission the monolith expands the mind of the hominid. The scene moves to where the hominid is contemplating a pile of bones, and then, in that moment, light flashes in his eyes, and he becomes aware of the possibility of using a jawbone as a weapon. (He sees himself in his imagination actually killing animals.)

The group then use this discovery to hunt for food, killing and eating meat rather than scrabbling for edible roots and leaves. This discovery (and perhaps the change in their nutrition) leads to attacking and killing with these weapons the hominid group that had occupied the water hole. I realized how this act forever transformed our relationship to the natural world. With a single leap of imagination, we had divorced ourselves from a passive coexistence to become the species that would dominate the world.

Then the proverbial light of realization switched on, and I knew that this coding to dominate was embedded in our primordial ancestors well before *Homo sapiens* evolved. It is the distinctive characteristic separating us from other primates, the drive to dominate nature. Sadly, this made sense, and I felt that humanity would always be impelled by this inborn code, regardless of any attempt to mitigate it through social or cultural mores; the impetus to dominate would always be there. I understood that this was the root evil behind the homicidal insanity of belligerent conquest and war that has been a plague on humanity since time immemorial.

The vision suddenly metamorphosed, and I was sitting in a forest clearing among a gathering of people in a circle. We were sharing the anguish, mourning the loss of the compassionate bond between humanity, the biosystem, and the sentient cosmos. Behind each person I could see other people, more incorporeal, and the circle of the living was the innermost part of an immense series of concentric circles of people who had lived before us. We were an intrinsic portion of the spiral of life, and then the exquisitely soft and sensual voice of the spirit of ayahuasca spoke to me: "and we are an evolving jewel in the maelstrom of creation."

I was shown how we could teach our children to redress this imbalance. I saw adults instructing children about our place in the immense web of life and how humans, other animals, and plants are each an element in nature. The vision revealed an immeasurable cosmic tapestry, with all life woven like gems into its fabric. Then the voice of the spirit said that the period of perceived separation from the natural world and the falsehood of domination that sets us above nature are going to change. A new dream of interconnection with the spiritual forces that underlie the natural world is already unfolding. People will be more and more drawn to explore their inner selves and discover a sense of community with other people and subsequently with all sentient life.

I understood that this was the potential direction of humanity, and I had the inescapable sensation that maybe the domination code embedded in our DNA could eventually be erased from our collective. In the ongoing evolution of consciousness of our species, the time has come to transform the competitive, dominant predisposition that has brought us to the brink of ecological devastation and to fashion a balanced, cooperative, and creative existence. This will take generations to realize, but the metamorphosis has already begun. This was a beautiful revelation, and it has certainly given me hope and a long-term optimistic outlook.

The following day, swinging gently to and fro on my hammock, I realized that Kubrick was an absolute genius, and of course he purposefully envisaged the analogies in his movie to explore the potential evolutionary destiny of humanity. To me his movie is an unparalleled prophetic vision. I see that the monolith is a metaphor for the higher order universal field of consciousness, and hallucinogenic plants allow us to enter into communion with this consciousness. Without a doubt the monolith can be seen as an analogy for ayahuasca as it spreads out from its rainforest home to bring illumination, healing, spiritual well-being, and a new sense of interconnectivity with life. I recommend *2001: A Space Odyssey* without hesitation to those who are working with mind-expanding plants and practices.

The plant teachers can show us how to transcend linear time itself, to journey within the eternal now to the very place in time where we experienced a difficult event or suffered a troubled period in our life. We can reexperience this, albeit from a different perspective, learn what happened, the reasons why it occurred, and the subsequent impact and consequences on our life, and then release any pain and trauma locked within our being. This release within the ayahuasca experience is called *la purga,* or the purge, when we literally purge this pain from our being. We release not only the contents of our stomach but also the deeply stored bile and sourness in our bodies generated from these difficult events. The plants offer us the potential for deep soul healing so we can become stronger and more able to engage fully in the precious gift of life.

Westerners have a disturbing tendency, in my view, to project a form of guruship onto shamans. Traditional shamans are not prepared culturally or psychologically for this type of adulation. Making shamans into superstars is damaging and can reveal the dark underbelly of human nature. This is an invitation to malpractice and abusive behavior that is ultimately destructive.

In general, the two main distinguishing characteristics of shamans are their mastery of expanded states of consciousness and their ability to establish a relationship with the transpersonal forces that we call spirits. Because of this relationship, which comes through a rigorous apprenticeship and self-discipline, they are able to harness the spiritual forces to serve their community.

When asked to describe the role of a shaman, *mestizo** shaman Javier Arevalo replied, "He learns everything about the rain forest and uses that knowledge to heal his people since they do not have money for Western style doctors. He uses Ayahuasca to discover in his visions, which plants will be effective for which illnesses."[3]

Amazonian shamans work with the everyday prosaic mess of life, illness, curses, and *saldera,* meaning a pervasive run of bad luck. Good luck and bad luck are not regarded as purely chance. Local people come to see shamans to find out why they are unable to find work, to discover

---

*Mestizo* indicates a person of mixed European and native ancestry, as opposed to a person who belongs to an indigenous community.

if their partner is cheating on them, or to receive a remedy for illness. They do not come to seek answers to deep questions about the transcendent nature of reality.

I am using the word *shaman* loosely in the narrative; the term *shaman*, or in Peru, *chaman*, originates in the Turkic Asiatic word šaman. The term *shaman* is a recent Western import into the Amazon in the past thirty years. In the Amazonian tradition there are many specializations and categories. The traditional generic term would be *vegetalista*, which denotes they have received their power from the plant kingdom. There are many subspecializations of the vegetalista, for example, *palero*, a specialist in the bark and roots of trees; *perfumero*, a specialist in the perfumes of plants and flowers; and *ayahuasquero*, a specialist in ayahuasca.

Iquitos, the capital city in the department of Loreto in the Amazon rainforest, has developed into a veritable mecca for those seeking the ayahuasca experience. Until the road to Natua was finally completed in 2007, there were no roads to the city, and the only route to get there was by airplane or river boat. The city in the nineteenth century was the center of the rubber industry, but by the early twentieth century, the rubber boom was over and the trade had moved to the Far East. The city had fallen into neglect and disrepair. It is now a place without an apparent purpose, resplendent in its postcolonial splendor literally in the middle of nowhere, a true frontier town. It is still an exhilarating experience standing on the esplanade called the Malecon at the edge of the city, overlooking the river, and knowing that some three thousand miles of rainforest is spread before you.

One thing I witnessed at close hand in the region around Iquitos is the effect caused by the *relatively* substantial influx of money into the shamanic and jungle lodge economy. To put it into perspective, Cusco receives hundreds of thousands tourists a year, and Iquitos just a few thousand. Even so, ayahuasca has become big money in the poor and impoverished region, in effect creating a small-scale "gold rush." This is not mass tourism by any means, but the revenue has created an imbalance in what was (and still is) the traditional niche vocation of the shaman. I reject the term *ayahuasca tourism;* it is pejorative and neither values nor respects the traveler's motivation, which I consider to be a pilgrimage or quest for healing and enlightenment. Nevertheless, an ayahuasca economy has sprung up, and visitors should not suspend their cognitive faculties and allow shamans and their associates to exploit their inner desires and personal aspirations.

I was present when a shaman offered to solve a woman's family problems by supplying a bottle of holy water collected from seven churches for 500 soles (the official currency in Peru is the sol, plural soles; 500 soles is around $180 in U.S. currency). I calculated it would have been the work of an hour and at most would cost him 5 soles in a *motokar* (a motorcycle-rickshaw) to dash around to seven churches. Placed within the context of a daily wage in the region, which is 20 to 50 soles, it shows how payment for shamanic assistance has been distorted. Fortunately, the woman said she would think about it, so I had an opportunity to take her aside and discuss it. The deal did not sit right with her, and she intuitively knew that it was not kosher.

Not everyone is as intuitive as this woman. At another meeting a woman loudly complained of her husband's inability to raise an erection. She started to laugh and then described in detail his problem in an acerbic and sarcastic tone. The shaman promised to prepare a special elixir for her husband, guaranteed to resolve this problem. The following day the shaman turned up asking the exorbitant price of 500 soles for a bottle of special elixir. She asked him what the ingredients were; he was completely taken aback by this question and was at a loss for words.

However, as it happens, the previous day I had looked into this matter and had discovered that he had not personally made the elixir; he had subcontracted the task to another shaman and paid him 15 soles. I had asked the subcontractor about the contents. I was therefore in a position to help the shaman out of his awkward situation, as he would have lost some serious face. I prompted him by naming each ingredient in the elixir, and I also mentioned some nonexistent constituents, such as *pene del mono* (monkey's penis); he nodded his head with enthusiasm to each ingredient. It was clear that he had not a clue what was in this elixir and had not even taken the trouble to ask the shaman who had made it on his behalf. I negotiated the price for the elixir to a reasonable 25 soles while the woman proudly held the bottle and continued her sarcastic invective about her husband. Listening to this disparaging rant I knew that if I was in her husband's place, I wouldn't want to get it up either.

I was disappointed at this rip-off. I had known this shaman since the 1990s, and he had always acted in a helpful and trustworthy manner, but over the years I saw how adulation and money had gone to his head. This kind of situation does happen; it's best to acknowledge it and move on, and so I decided not to work with him again. As a side note, although we tend to regard the concept of "losing face" as primarily Asian in origin, in Peru it is also significant. If you force an issue and thereby cause a Peruvian to lose face, that person will not be well-disposed toward you, and you may even make an enemy. It is in your best interests to avoid this, even though you may be in the right; smile if as nothing has happened, move on, and let it go.

Sometimes shamanic situations in the region do get serious. For instance, a friend of mine who had accompanied me to a few ayahuasca ceremonies in the Amazon got into a dangerous situation when she went on a solo trip. One of her endearing characteristics is that she is forever complaining about everything. It has never bothered me. I see it as a sort of surreal comedy, and I find the whole thing amusing; in fact, I would be concerned if she wasn't complaining because then something for certain could be amiss. On her solo visit she went to a lodge to drink ayahuasca, but there her complaining was not welcome. She was not happy and complained about the food, the insects, the accommodations, and the weather, and she demanded a refund of her money (which she had paid up front). The lodge owner said that wouldn't be a problem, and he would give her a refund the following day.

That evening she attended the ayahuasca ceremony. The shaman came over to her, made some *sopladas,** and chanted ícaros. The next thing she knew, she was waking up by the side of the Iquitos to Nauta road (quite some distance away), in her underwear, with her passport tucked into her underpants. This is awful and shocking without a doubt, but it could have been a hell of a lot worse. It would have been just as easy for these people to take her out on a boat, weigh her down, and dump her into the river, where she would be fish food. It was a horrific ordeal, but she was lucky. She was too intimidated to report this to the police, and even if she had, it would have led nowhere because the charge would have been denied, and there was no concrete evidence. Even if she'd had a solid case, the owner would have encouraged the police to drop the matter.

Unfortunately, these vexing situations do happen, so be careful if you are on your own. At the end of the day, you are in "Wild West" frontier territory. I have had my run-ins with the police there; not much you can do except grit your teeth, smile, pay up, and move on.†

I'd like to add a cautionary note on the importance of knowing what is in the ayahuasca brew. Some shamans add to the ayahuasca the plant called *toé* (*Brugmansia suaveolens*), also known locally as *tomapende* or

---

*Soplada* is the Spanish word for "to blow." *Soplo,* or *soplada,* usually refers to the practice of blowing mapacho (tobacco) smoke onto a person. The soplada is an important part of healing and is typically used for cleansing and as a conduit for the shaman's concentration and energy.

†There are some good resources on the Internet regarding safety while undertaking an ayahuasca experience. I recommend Steve Beyer's informative blog at www.singingtotheplants.com/2012/05/traveling-safely-to-drink-ayahuasca.

In addition, research the medical contraindications regarding ayahuasca and any prescription drugs you may be taking, such as selective serotonin reuptake inhibitors (SSRIs), typically used as antidepressants (for example, Prozac and Seroxat). There is a comprehensive list of contraindications of pharmaceutical medications and herbs at www.ayahuascasafety.org. I also recommend that you follow the traditions and taboos around ayahuasca. They have been in place for thousands of years and are a well and truly tried body of practices. I have addressed this important topic in the book *Plant Spirit Shamanism,* published by Destiny Books in 2006.

*floripondio*. Brugmansia is a psychoactively dangerous deliriant with toxic anticholinergic effects that wreak havoc with the human nervous system and mental faculties, and can lead to a horrendous experience in extremis. Shamans do work with toé even though it has a shady reputation because of its use for *brujeria*.* There are valid reasons why a shaman needs knowledge of the plant if he is to heal victims of the *brujos* who use toé for harmful purposes.

In my view, adding toé to the ayahuasca brew without informing people is very irresponsible. I have had trouble on two occasions with this. On one of these, I knew the shaman and gave him the money for the brew, but the problem (as I later found out) was that he had not made the brew himself and was thus ignorant of its contents. We drank the ayahuasca concoction, and after a half hour or so the shaman went into a panic, muttering toé and holding his hand over his mouth so his vomit wouldn't spray everywhere, and he along with the two other participants in the ceremony ran out of the ceremonial cabin locally known as a *maloka*. I sat there abandoned in the dark with the effect of the brew gradually increasing and realized that I could be in seriously deep shit. Even thinking that one could be in a tight spot in these circumstances is in itself dangerous, so I avoided going into a negative spiral of thinking. I decided that I would be better off in my hut, but in hindsight that was maybe not such a great idea. To this day I have no idea how I made it back to the hut. My vision was an unfocused blur; I could neither see nor walk straight. I staggered through the jungle, bumped into trees, tripped over logs, and pushed my way through dense bushes, and the following day I was covered in scratches and a myriad of insect bites. I desperately wanted to vomit to get the brew out of me, but even though I tried, I couldn't. Anyway, somehow I made it back to the hut, laid down on

---

*Brujeria* is the Spanish word for "witchcraft." A *brujo* (masculine) or *bruja* (feminine), meaning "sorcerer" or "witch," can invoke malign forces to harm another person by preparing concoctions that clients can introduce secretly into a victim's food, drink, or bathwater.

the bed, and then one of the longest and weirdest nights of my life began.

I heard a loud crunching sound coming from the toilet. I sat up and saw a group of huge rats eating the toilet bowl, and suddenly I heard a loud splash and an anaconda reared up from the bowl, grabbed one of the rats in its mouth, and withdrew into the bowl. This looked so real, I was not even sure if it was a hallucination, so I got off the bed, slammed the bathroom door shut, and barricaded it with my bags and whatever else was at hand. I was too scared to go to the toilet that night.

Then with a rushing noise, I found myself out of my body, fully conscious, and cognizant in a half-luminous, eerie jungle. I cannot accurately describe the distinctive quality of the illumination. It was neither dark nor light, but a metallic pewter color, and my body was translucent silver. To either side were massive *lianas* (vines) hanging down from the trees, twisting and moving like snakes. The leaves on the bushes rustled, and the bushes made whispering sounds as if talking to each other. I heard the sounds of animals and watched the floating, flickering lights of firefly clusters, which was mesmerizing. At times I sensed a jaguar stalking me. This was unnerving, and I kept on looking back to see if I was being followed. At one point the pathway became a gigantic serpent, a *sachamama,* winding its way through the jungle, and it felt as if I was on a living, undulating conveyor belt.

I knew I was somewhere, but in a strange supernatural somewhere. I was gripped by a mixture of total fascination and anxiety, and at times waves of icy fear moved through me. I was certainly uneasy, to say the least, but I was very aware that this would be a very bad moment to come unglued. If that happened I would be absolutely and unequivocally fucked. I started to think about the difficulty that I had in getting back into my body during my previous toé experience, many years earlier, but on that occasion I had some help, and here I was on my own. It was critical to master my thoughts and not allow them to spin down into a maelstrom of hysteria.

I stopped walking, and marshaled my thoughts and feelings. I started to focus on the joyful, funny, and beautiful things in my life, and I recalled the silly songs about polar bears, elephants, and kangaroos I used to make up and sing to my daughters when they were little. I felt as if I was drawing them to me. My spirits lifted, I became calm, and then I knew with certainty that I would get out of my difficulty. I smiled and sang the Animals song "We Gotta Get Out of This Place." Then suddenly I was not there; I was back in my hut lying on the bed. I assume that I had fallen asleep (although I really can't be sure of that), because I awoke feeling a very heavy weight on top of me. I opened an eye and saw a very large snake coiled on me. I thought, "Don't panic. . . . You are hallucinating. . . . This is not happening." I was really trying hard not to freak out because it looked and felt so palpable. I laid there for what felt like hours without making the slightest movement to keep from disturbing the large and heavy snake lying on top of me.

Somehow I must have fallen into actual, bona fide sleep because when I awoke it was daytime. The snake was not there, and I saw my bags piled up against the bathroom door. I tiptoed to the door and gently opened it. The rats had also gone, and the toilet bowl, to my surprise, was unchewed. I felt exhausted, dehydrated, and generally wasted, something that I don't get with ayahuasca. I took my water bottle and sat outside sipping it. The water tasted like the nectar of the gods; it was the best water I had ever drunk in my life; it was beyond exquisite; it was sublime. That was one of my toé experiences; yes, it was interesting, but it's not one that I would care to repeat. Later in the morning I returned to the maloka, found the bottle of ayahuasca, and emptied out the remaining dregs on the earth outside. There was a lot to reflect on: I had experienced a subjective reality through the meshing of my mind and senses, and I had entered the mythological world of the Amazon and it felt completely real. It was if a Pablo Amaringo painting had come to life.

It is critical that you know what is in the ayahuasca brew. If the shaman prevaricates, that is a sign that he does not know what plants have been added, which means he bought it from another shaman or from the market. You really need to be very fussy about this, and if the information is not forthcoming, then I would personally decline to drink it. It really is best if you are present at the actual brewing of the ayahuasca. Aside from the admixture issue, being present and participating in the brewing is a rewarding and meaningful experience.

Entheogens like ayahuasca are catalysts for spiritual insights and offer direct encounters with the great mystery. In this exploration, safety is an important matter, but also keep in mind that it is an adventure, and in my view it is good to have adventures, to boldly go and all that. Adventures keep you young, and an adventure standing prominent above the mundane gives life additional meaning.

In November 2007, I had an extraordinary, momentous, and reality-shattering experience. I was in the Amazon at Mishana, living in my cabin or *tambo* at the edge of the River Nanay (see color plate 10). Mishana is part of the Allpahuayo-Mishana Nature Reserve, about three hours by boat from Iquitos. One morning around dawn, I was roused from my sleep by a resounding and deep bass sound like a foghorn. I jumped out of the hammock to find out what it was, and there in the river was one of the most amazing things that I had ever seen, an enormous *pucabufeo* (pink dolphin) leaping out of the water. I was spellbound watching this wonderful creature with its dusky red color diving into the river, disappearing from sight and then suddenly bursting out of the water further along. Then it submerged for a few minutes, and just when I thought it had swum away, suddenly it shot out of the water right in front of me. As I watched it soared and rolled through the air before diving back in. Then it was gone and did not return.

This was one of the most awesome events that I have witnessed in my life. I had seen the gray Amazonian dolphins along the Nanay, but never a pucabufeo. Later, still buzzing with excitement, I met up with the others in the group at breakfast in our big house with a deck called the *casa grande*. I was surprised that no one else had heard or seen the huge pink dolphin. I never imagined that a pink dolphin could be that large; I had read that they grew to two meters in length, but this dolphin was the size of a large car. That was a sensational start to the day, yet I had no inkling of what would lie ahead in the next twenty-four hours.

That evening we were having an ayahuasca ceremony with a skilled Shipibo shaman named Enrique, with whom we had worked before. There was also José, a Huitoto shaman who had been working with a group the previous week and was staying over for a few days. (The Huitoto are another group of Peruvian Indians.) A few years earlier I had stayed at a Huitoto village when I was traveling around with Chuck, an ayahuasca buddy from Oakland, California. We hung out at the hut of Mario, the village chief, and were made very welcome. The Huitoto were very hospitable and affable. The ayahuasca ceremonies were different than what I was used to, as instead of sitting or lying down we were on hammocks, which I really liked. Mario played the *arpa de duendes* (a wooden stringed instrument) with great gusto, and the ayahuasca was different too, having *chiricsango* (*Brunfelsia grandiflora*), *guayusa* (*Ilex guayusa*), and ajo sacha added to the usual brew of ayahuasca vine and chacruna. I did drink ayahuasca with José and his group, but for some reason he preferred to hold the ceremony in an enclosed space with the group having plastic bowls to vomit in. This for me was a bit icky. Purging is important in ayahuasca because it is not just the contents of your stomach that are discharged (from either end) but deeply buried emotional trauma, toxic energies, and disease. So if you are going to purge, get out there and give it all to nature. Your purge is a deep cleansing, a purifying gift from ayahuasca, and throwing up into a bucket or a toilet bowl for me is definitely disgusting.

In the evening, before the ceremony started, I was relaxing in a hammock in the large open area overlooking the river when I noticed José come in and go to the table where the bottle of ayahuasca was standing. He opened the ayahuasca bottle, did a soplo, sang an ícaro to the ayahuasca, resealed the bottle, and went away. It did strike me as odd, and I had an uneasy feeling, but I was so languid in the jungle heat lying in the hammock that I did not follow up on my misgivings and inform Enrique, who was holding the ceremony. By ignoring my intuition I made a big mistake.

Around an hour later we started the ceremony. That evening we were drinking a very potent form of the brew known as *yagé*, made with *chaliponga* (*Diplopterys cabrerana*), not chacruna.* Enrique sang his ícaro with the ayahuasca, and we all drank. However, within twenty minutes or so things went awry. I watched as Enrique vomited the ayahuasca, and I knew without a doubt that something was not right. An experienced Shipibo shaman does not vomit, and certainly never after such a short time. Enrique left the maloka, went to the riverbank, and started to howl like a wounded animal. As I listened to the howling I realized that he had lost his mind and that we were in for an extremely rough ride that night.

Suddenly a storm erupted, without warning. Usually you know that a storm is coming: the wind picks up and the rain draws close, sounding like an approaching train. These warning signs allow you to stow away your gear, unhook the hammock, and all that. However, this massive thunderstorm just appeared out of the blue. No rain fell at all, and lightning flashed everywhere. Lightning bolts hit just one hundred yards away. By this time the yagé had set in, and it was so strong that I could not move. Even if I could have moved there was nowhere to go and nowhere to hide.

The moment before each lightning flash, I got a strong electric shock that lasted a few seconds, and then I was thrown out of my body. I had to use maximum determination and strength to return to my body, and then I would violently purge. I was unable to move, so I just leaned

---

*Chaliponga is used in the ayahuasca brew known as yagé, typically from the Ecuadorian and Colombian Amazon. Chaliponga is much stronger and contains five times more tryptamines than chacruna.

over my chair and threw up on the floor. The storm continued to rage, and as it grew more intense the mareación also grew in intensity.

The lightning came closer and closer from over the river, the electric shocks got stronger, and then I realized that I would die there. I knew that I faced imminent death. It would be an ignominious death; I would be a burnt and blistered lump of flesh and bone.

This would be worse than death; it would be complete annihilation. In that moment I prepared to die. This was not a conscious act; it was an act of my soul. Images of my life did not flash by, but I relived and reexperienced an all-consuming emotional pain and sadness that stemmed from the beginning of my life. I had forgotten how awful and wretched I had felt when I was young, I shuddered and went into contortions as I reenacted the excruciating pain. I felt tortured. Then the agonizing pain rose through my body, and I purged over the side of my chair.

I knew each thought could be my final one. My sense of time altered, from a continual flow of movement and events into a procession of distinct, infinitesimal moments. It was like watching a movie frame by single frame. I faced my ultimate fear—not of death, but of total oblivion. I watched as the sky tore into shreds, and I saw what I had assumed to be reality going through a cosmic shredding machine.

This extraordinary situation continued while I was still getting electric shocks and the lightning struck all around me. I reached out through my mind and felt that I could telepathically communicate with my loved ones. I said farewell and felt unbearable guilt about abandoning my two daughters in this awful way. I reexperienced nightmares from when I was a child; that nightmare world was in my "here and now" reality. The nightmares were purged too.

The storm went on for hours, unmoving in its location overhead, unvarying in its savage intensity. Then in the distance I heard Enrique chanting ícaros; he had broken through his torment and had come back. As he chanted, the storm became less severe and started to depart. He came over to me, and all I could see of him was a ball of shimmering, luminescent threads. He chanted ícaros to me for a long time, and I felt the vibrations of the ícaros resonate in my deepest being, through every fiber of my body. Then I was transformed. When I stood up, I had become transparent, and I could see within my body. I saw the obnoxious and nauseating mass of the brujeria that had been sent to me. This fetid energy released from me in a burst of rainbow light. It was by now dawn; the most fearful night of my life had metamorphosed into the most transcendentally beautiful experience of my life.

After Enrique had chanted to the four other people in the ceremony, a tangible sense of peace descended. As the sun rose in the sky, we sat and shared our experiences; those present that evening had faced our personal nemesis or greatest fear. For Enrique it was losing contact with God. I had experienced an existential fear that went beyond the aspiration to avoid death or pain; it was a deep-rooted dread that what I recognized as "I" would cease to exist. I also realized that at last I understood ayahuasca. I had drunk the brew at least two hundred or more times, but only now did I get it. Ayahuasca was not only an *other* consciousness, but in an ineffable way an intrinsic part of the fabric of reality itself.

Later in the day I checked in with Marcio, who was assisting at the ceremony and did not drink ayahuasca. I asked him if there really was a storm. He laughed as if I was crazy and replied, "Yes, for sure!" Two days later, my colleague Peter Cloudsley came with the boat carrying supplies from Iquitos. When he joined us, he picked up on the atmosphere and asked, "What's happened?" All I could say was "I could tell you what happened, but then I can't tell you what happened." Peter quickly got the drift. Even after all those years, I am still working on what took place that night. To tie up a loose end, José, the Huitoto shaman, had left Mishana the night before. I also poked around and found out that there had been some acrimony between him and Enrique. Of course, in the Amazon there would be no way to get to the bottom of this kind of situation, so I just left it.

Later I discussed this experience with Pablo Amaringo, and he said that the storm was an appearance of the Huairamama, the legendary Mother of the Air. This kind of storm in the Amazon—with powerful winds, thunder and lightning, but no rain—is known as a *supay-cato* or *supay-qat'a*. This is a Quechua phrase meaning either "supernatural bath" or "supernatural cloud."

In retrospect, my experiences with entheogens have enriched and transformed my life. They have been a conduit to a realm of consciousness that I term the Great Domain. In this realm we are an intrinsic aspect of an infinite spirit or mind. In this domain we see that our experience of separateness is an illusion generated by being in a bodily vehicle that houses our senses. Our consciousness simultaneously permeates both the physical and spirit realms. In the Great Domain there is only the one emotion of ecstatic bliss, and here in the physical world we undergo a process of spiritual and emotional development that informs and illuminates this great mind. If this is God, then we are a part of it, and we also participate in its evolution.

Many of my visionary experiences with ayahuasca have led to a deeper understanding of my life and the role that various people had played in it. Sometimes in visions I became those people, lived their lives, and came to understand why they did what they did, and the decisions they had to make in their lives. These revelatory experiences invariably led to some form of closure with that person, like completing a chapter or healing my relationship with that person.

As ayahuasca enters the mainstream its perception in the Western mind is changing from a traditional body of indigenous practices into a new form. In this new form, it is viewed as a remedy for psychological ailments such as PTSD, clinical depression, and drug addiction. The organization founded by Rick Doblin, the Multidisciplinary Association for Psychedelic Studies (MAPS), is currently developing protocols for therapy in conjunction with the FDA. Research papers on this topic are available online at the MAPS website. These protocols apply not only to ayahuasca but to other hallucinogens as well, such as psilocybin (the psychoactive alkaloid in certain mushrooms).

The entry of ayahuasca into the Western mind has also led to a clash of perspectives. Some perceive ayahuasca and other psychotropic plants from a reductionist perspective; crudely put, ayahuasca is regarded as orally taken DMT liquid. I believe that this view is misguided for two main reasons. First, the ayahuasca brew contains many other alkaloids, and all work together in a chemical harmony. Figuratively speaking, isolating DMT in the mix is like separating the string section out of a symphony orchestra; you still hear the tune but the harmonious interaction between the various groups of instruments is lost. Second, the "liquid DMT" view also excludes the spiritual dimension, the sense that you are interacting or in communion with another field of transcendent spiritual consciousness.

I can add a small observation: ayahuasca is also becoming personified as the "mother," or "madre." It seems to be our nature to make the phrase "the Word was made flesh, and dwelt among us" into something tangible rather than perceive it as a metaphor for something unknowable. My experience is that ayahuasca is beyond the male/female dichotomy; it is something "other" that in some way is part of the fabric of reality, and I personally wouldn't regard reality as being either male or female.

## EXERCISE

## ✳ Developing and Exploring Your Connection to the Plant Spirits

Traditional cultures regard plants as alive and conscious. Although this worldview is ridiculed in Western culture, many Westerners are aware of a spiritual connection to the world of plants and search for ways to create a profound connection with the plant kingdom.

The first and possibly the most important key in developing your relationship with a plant spirit (and what really helps to "open the door" or make the connection work) is cultivating a benign attitude and good intentions toward the plant. Our rational mind is not an ally in this endeavor, so avoid trying to understand what is happening. Go with your feelings; don't dismiss them.

The idea is to perceive the world around us in a new and different way. When we were children, the world was novel and untarnished, and as we grew up, the world lost its freshness and novelty. When you enter into communion with a plant, try to evoke that childlike manner of perceiving the world, fostering a new and pristine vision, which many of us have lost in life's maelstrom of banality.

The plant consciousness, or spirit, communicates with us when we are in a relaxed, gentle, trancelike state. Moving into this altered state of consciousness can be achieved gently, for example, by walking at a slow and steady pace through a forest, woodland, or park. Gradually the rhythm of this slow and steady movement will bring you into a heightened state of awareness. When you sense this subtle shift, lift up your eyes and look around. Allow yourself to be drawn to whatever tree, bush, or plant attracts your attention; you may experience this attraction as akin to a little "tug."

Now go and sit with the plant. Use all your sensory and tactile faculties to engage with the plant. The following exercises will help you along.

**Visual.** Study the shape and form of the plant. Does it grow alone or in a cluster? Look at the form of the leaves, and look at the spaces between the leaves and branches (the forms within the forms). This practice is called *gazing,* which offers a way to perceive patterns outside the consensually agreed shapes and forms.

**Smell.** Our olfactory nerves go directly into the region of the brain called the limbic system. The limbic system is also called our primitive brain because its structure is below the linguistic and higher functions of the cerebral cortex. The limbic system is the location of our primal (unconscious) emotions and needs. The sense of smell is our only sense that has this access to our primal mind. Breathe in the fragrance of the plant and allow any feelings, memories, images, and associations to arise and be experienced.

**Tactile.** Tactile awareness involves our sense of touch. Gently move your hand toward the plant. Can you discern any movement or sense a connection between your energy field and that of the plant? Touch the leaves or bark with your fingers. You may sense the flow of energy from within the plant down into the earth and up into the sky.

**Taste.** Place a very small piece of the plant against your tongue and gently taste it. The taste may be acrid, bitter, hot, sweet, sour, or sharp. The taste may attract you or repel you, or your reaction may be completely neutral. This tasting will give you an indication of its character or "personality." Exercise caution with this practice because some plants are toxic. Do not eat or swallow the plant.

When you have completed these practices (which form part of the Amazonian plant apprenticeship, the diet), take time to meditate or embark on a shamanic journey to encounter the spirit of the plant you have been working with.

Although I lean toward the traditional view and use of ayahuasca, as it transforms and meets the Western mind, I too have to embrace this change. In other words, *tempora mutantur, nos et mutamur in illis* (times change, and we change with them). However I do feel that there is so much we can learn and discover from the indigenous peoples, not only about the medicinal properties of plants, but also about communication between humans and plant consciousness.

# 11

# HEALING AND SORCERY IN THE PHILIPPINES AND PERU

*Even chance meetings are the result of karma. . . . Things in life are fated by our previous lives. That even in the smallest events there's no such thing as coincidence.*

HARUKI MURAKAMI, *KAFKA ON THE SHORE*

My first visit to the Philippines was in 1998. I was intrigued by the phenomenon of *psychic surgery,* or *bare-hand surgery,* after meeting a Philippines healer the previous year in England. I could not have guessed that this would be the beginning of an enthralling adventure into the enigmatic and capricious world of the Philippines spirit healer.

The Philippines is an archipelago of seven thousand islands with a myriad of cultures; it boasts 120 recognized languages. The country still bears the stamp of the former colonial powers, Spain and later the United States, following the Spanish–American War in 1898. The

American occupation led to English being a lingua franca (side by side with Tagalog).

The ancestral traditions and the strong folk culture of the Philippines have fostered a climate of tolerance and acceptance toward traditional healers, shamans, and psychic surgeons. This tolerance had been taken up by government ministers, presidents, and, interestingly, the powerful Catholic Church. A sympathetic feature article entitled "Priest Heals through Power of Touch," featuring Father Fernando Saurez, was printed in the national newspaper.[1] He came to national prominence in part because the husband of President Arroyo was healed by the priest in his celebrated "miraculous recovery." Father Saurez's healing work is all approved and praised by the church hierarchy.

Filipino traditions have maintained an awareness and faith in the existence of *anitos,* the nature spirits that reside between the natural and supernatural worlds. Although the Filipino people broadly regard themselves as rationalists, they more readily embrace the more intangible, enigmatic, and metaphysical *magical reality.*

The situation is comparable to Peru. Since the Spanish conquest and colonization five hundred years ago, the folk customs and spiritual practices have not been eradicated, despite the early Catholic missionaries holding the native practices in considerable contempt. As in the Philippines, there has been a syncretism of traditional lore and the Church. For instance, the Andean *ofrenda* ceremony (providing an offering to the nature spirits, or *apu*) is incorporated in the liturgy.

In the Philippines, there is the ambition to move into a modern "shopping mall" and "gated community" society. This is literally marketed as the "Philippines Dream," but this dream is only relevant in the modern cities. The vast majority of people live in a more rural environment. There is also a vast gap in wealth between the urban middle class and those in the provincial rural areas. The people who live in the remote rural settlements and outer provinces maintain their language and ethnic traditions. There is often a considerable distance from modern medical facilities and little money to pay for modern medical treatment and medication. This means that there is still a lot of work for the traditional healers, such as the *albularyos* (shamans), *herbolarios* (herb doctors), and *manghihilot* (traditional bonesetters). I find it refreshingly interesting that the Philippines enjoys a mercurial mixture of folk traditions and indigenous shamanism side by side with the modern Western outlook.

The bare-hand surgeons, or psychic surgeons, of the Philippines are one of the most enduring enigmas of modern times. Much controversy has surrounded these so-called miracle healers. Their ability to open people's bodies with their hands defies consensual reality. How can a human body open and close by touch? How can solid objects become permeable to allow a hand to move through them? It really does require an incredible leap of the imagination to entertain the idea that this phenomenon exists. It is a challenge to our sensibilities and to our thinking. I can understand that this is dismissed as weird and superstitious nonsense, and that the bare-hand healers are seen as charlatans skilled in sleight of hand.

The journey for me started on the opposite side of the world, in Peru, and I had no inkling of the peculiar circumstances that would propel me into the extraordinary world of sorcery and psychic surgery in the Philippines. In 1999, I was returning to Lima from the Amazon rainforest, where I had been working with ayahuasca. As I disembarked from the airplane, it felt as if I was hit by a bolt of lightning. The force of it was so strong that my knees buckled, the world spun around me, and the clamor of the airport became silent. I came close to fainting but managed to grip the rail of the stairs to prevent falling down on the tarmac.

I later flew back to England and returned to my house in Brighton, and there, day by day, my condition deteriorated. My left hand grew weak and numb, and it became difficult to do simple, everyday tasks, such as buttoning up my trousers. Paralysis gradually spread upward along my arm, and I became increasingly fatigued; it was difficult to walk up the hill to my house. I saw my doctor, but when I described my symptoms he just shrugged his shoulders in bewilderment. The situation continued to deteriorate, my left eye closed, and the left side of my mouth and tongue became numb. I had difficulty breathing. I did not know what to do, and I was at my wits' end. Then, one night, I had a dream in which the Tibetan Lama appeared, and he very gently said, "Go to the Philippines. You will get help there." I awoke, and without a shadow of doubt, I knew I would go.

I traveled to the Philippines with a friend and colleague, the holistic health practitioner Patrick Hamouy. There we visited the healer we had met in 1998, and although he gave encouraging words, it was clear that he could not help me. Later that evening, I met a man named John at the hotel where we were staying. He told me that he came to the Philippines every few years to see Brother Roger, a healer living in Baguio. John told me that he had been suffering from severe Parkinson's disease. At times it was so bad that it was difficult to eat and drink because his arms would fling violently around and his head would uncontrollably jerk to and fro. However, for the past five years the problems had abated since he had been seeing the healer. I realized that this was the man I needed to see. The following morning, we took a bus that drove up through the scenic Cordillera mountain range to Baguio to meet the healer.

His "office" was a simple street-side café cum shop selling everything from shampoo sachets to the local boiled egg delicacy, which children buy in the dozens each week. The waiting room was the café itself, and his treatment room was a small curtained-off room at the back. We went into the treatment room, and he studied me carefully, and then he started to talk about Siquijor, an island in the Philippines archipelago. "This island has a fearsome reputation among ordinary Filipinos. This is the home to practitioners of sorcery and black magic." He continued, "The Mangkukulam [sorcerers] are paid by people who hold grudges and animosities to make a kulam [curse or evil eye] to harm the other person." I was thinking, "What is this about? Why is he telling me this?" I was soon to understand the reason. He said, "This is what has happened to you. A woman holds a deep resentment toward you, and she has paid a sorcerer to curse and destroy you."

He started the healing right away, and he said that in five days' time we would identify the perpetrator, referring to the originator of the curse rather than the sorcerer. This would allow the dark force to be released and sent back to its source. When he "operated" on me, his hand entered my body and removed an obnoxious mass of tissue from my wrist that had an uncanny resemblance to the tentacles of an octopus (figure 11.1). When I returned to the hotel, I enthusiastically told Patrick about the session, and from then on he joined me on the daily trips to Roger.

Over the next four days he continued to open my body and extract loathsome things from my arm and my neck along the left side of my body. Each time the effect was immediate: I felt stronger, energized, and more free. He instructed me to prepare for a ritual by compiling a list of all the women I had met in the past twelve months.

I finally managed to compile the list of names, sixty-five in total. On Friday, when we arrived at his café, he told me to buy an egg. I returned a few minutes later carefully holding the egg I had just bought for three pesos from a local store. In his treatment room, he had set up an altar on a large metal tray. On the altar stood an empty wine bottle, a bowl, plugs of local tobacco, and leaves of *bacchia* (*Dieffenbachia* sp.).

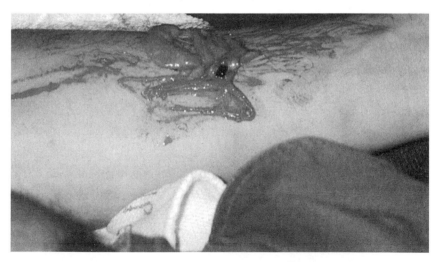

Figure 11.1. Mass of tissue removed from my arm
(Photo by Patrick Hamouy)

He asked me to tear the list into individual strips, with each strip holding a single name, fold them, and place them into the bottle. While I was carrying out this task, he left the room. He returned a few minutes later, went to the altar, and murmured his prayers and blessings. He then told me to take the egg and hold it above the neck of the bottle. He whispered an incantation and then lifted a bottle of gin, saying, "That was the only bottle of spirits that I have." Then he poured the gin over my hand that was holding the egg. As soon as that was done, he indicated that I should break the egg open into the bowl and look for the folded strip of paper. I used a toothpick to poke around, and then to my astonishment I saw a folded piece of paper inside the yolk.

I carefully teased the yolky paper strip open with the toothpick, and in my own handwriting was the name of a woman with whom I had had an affair in Peru. Something had worried me about her and made me uncomfortable. She had also become extremely possessive, and I had to end the relationship. When I met her to tell her this, she replied, "If I can't have you, then no one will." She said this in such an intense way that I shivered, and I immediately got up and left, greatly relieved to be out of the relationship—or so I had thought at the time.

I realized that this could have been a perfect murder and speculated about the number of people who have become victims and inexplicably died due to this malevolent type of sorcery. My assumption that rational Westerners who do not believe in the power of the dark arts would not get entangled in sorcery was obviously naive. The introspection and musing over, I felt like a new man and expressed my gratitude for his help. He said, "Do not thank me; thank the Holy Spirit. I am just a tool like a hammer, and it is the spirit who does all the healing."

Some final thoughts on this episode: I had no idea what the consequences would be for the woman who instigated this. In the ritual, as Brother Roger explained, the dark force would be returned to its source. A few years later, I was in Peru drinking a beer on a terrace, and I saw some distance away a woman walking in my direction. It was the peculiar way she was walking that grabbed my attention; her head was bowed down, and she was shielding the left side of her face with her arm. When she was opposite to me, I got a clearer view, and I saw that it was the woman from my past. I was shocked to see that the left side of her face was disfigured and covered in dark red blotches, and even in the tropical heat I shivered. I pondered a while on karma and on the ancient platitudes about not doing to others what you do not want done to yourself, and the message was clear: beware of messing with dark energy because it can come back to bite your ass.

There is interesting connection regarding the patterned leaves of *Dieffenbachia* that Brother Roger placed on the altar. In Peru this plant is known colloquially as *patiquina* and is used for protection against sorcery. If a shaman chants the ícaro of the plant, it then functions like a shield against *hechiceria,* a particularly malevolent form of sorcery that can kill a person. Pablo Amaringo in his paintings features patiquina in this context. The leaves of this plant are commonly used in floral baths to protect against sorcery.

My friend Patrick had followed a strict macrobiotic and vegetarian food regime for many years, yet still he was plagued by intestinal pains (from his earlier eating habits). His initial session with Brother Roger was incredible. I was standing close by as he made an opening in Patrick's abdomen, and inside I could see a tube. It was his descending colon, neatly sliced open, and from the lower open end he pulled out what appeared to be a twelve-inch-long piece of mummified turd; as I glanced back at the opening, it closed just like a camera shutter. A half hour later, as we were eating lunch, Patrick said that he had considered a conventional operation to remove the obstruction, but it would have required that the colon be stapled together, along with a three-month diet of liquid food, followed by another three months of baby food, and a further six months before eating what he wanted. Yet here we were half an hour later eating lunch.

I visited Brother Roger frequently over the next few years and organized groups to visit other Filipino healers and shamans. I asked him if there were any other healers in his family. He said "No," and added, "In many generations I am the only one with this gift." I asked him how he discovered this gift. He replied,

> As a young child I was often told that I would be "special" because I was a breech delivery, but I never knew or was told exactly what this special attribute was. I discovered the ability when I was thirteen when a neighboring boy the same age as me had swallowed a fishbone and became very ill. His neck became swollen and infected. He was unable to eat, and after two weeks his condition was getting very serious. Another neighbor brought me to the boy and asked me to heal him. I did not know what to do, so I just gently massaged the boy's neck, when suddenly my fingers moved inside the boy's throat. I was so shocked that I pulled away, and I found that I was holding the fishbone in my hand. I was so frightened, I thought I had killed the boy, so I run away and hid in the forest for three weeks.
>
> Later a friend found me and said that the boy was well and had recovered. I returned to my village, but I was no longer welcome because people thought I was a sorcerer and was "touched by the devil." I had been expelled from school, and even my parents had turned their backs on me. So I had to leave home and travel. It was a lonely and difficult period in my life because I was denounced when people found out who I was, so I had to keep moving.

He then lifted his shirt and showed me the whip scars on his back. "I was hounded and whipped with vines, which had thorns attached." He indicated a vase in his room in which he still kept the very same vines as a reminder of those times.

> I survived by grafting, selling cigarettes, cleaning shoes, and sleeping rough, living as an outcast. Eventually I earned enough money to enroll in school, and I could then get a job. I lost everything in the 1990 earthquake that devastated the city [Baguio], and so I moved to Manila, where I found work and started to rebuild my life. About seven years ago I returned to Baguio, opened the bodega, and started healing again.

I began to assist him in his practice, and he showed me how to work with the healing spirit. He said that the spirit would protect both the patient and me from any infection. He then demonstrated how it worked; grasping my hand he brought his hand above mine with his fingers extended above mine by a few inches (figure 11.2).

*See, it is as if my hand is the spirit hand. The spirit hand moves first by making the opening, and my hand follows. The spirit hand takes the diseased tissue and places it in my hand, and as I withdraw my hand, the spirit hand also withdraws. As this happens, the opening in the body closes. You see, I told you that I am just the instrument, and the spirit does all the healing.*

To see a person's body opening was one thing, but to actually place my hand in the person's body was an entirely different experience, evoking enormous anxiety. As I placed my fingers inside a man's groin, Roger asked me if I could feel the lumpy tissue. I said, "Yes," and he said, "Pull it out." I withdrew my hand and was looking at a piece of dead tissue,

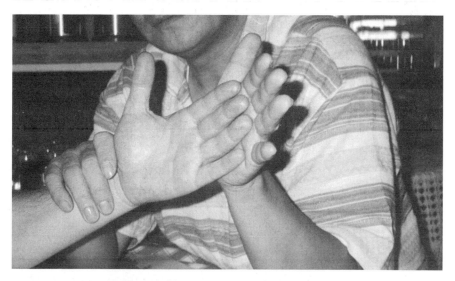

Figure 11.2. Demonstrating how the spirit hand connects with the physical hand (Photo by Patrick Hamouy)

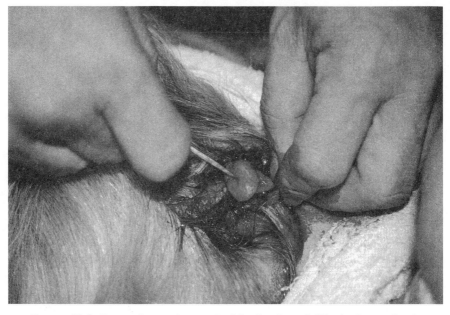

Figure 11.3. Removing a tumor inside the head (Photo by author)

which had come from his patient's prostate gland. The man had felt no pain or discomfort, and the opening in the groin had sealed. There were no markings or scars to indicate that a few moments previously it had been open.

He also showed me how to remove cataracts. To do this, I gently rubbed my finger over the person's eye for a few seconds (figure 11.4). I never came into direct contact with the eye itself because a soft substance rested between my finger and the eye, which was the healing spirit. The cataract was pushed to the edge, and then using a cotton swab I lifted it out and spread the membrane on a glass to show the patient (see color plate 11).

Belief in the existence of incorporeal beings is predominant in religions, folk stories, and shamanism, but it is still surprising when you directly encounter these beings in our material world. When we went to see the healer, we would first chat and drink tea, and then he would abruptly stand up, go to the treatment room, and begin. One day our initial tea drinking was taking longer than usual, and I asked him why

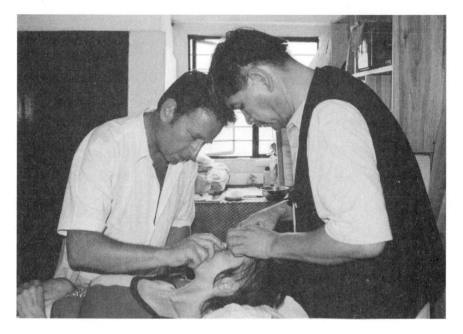

Figure 11.4. Removing cataracts from an eye (Photo by Patrick Hamouy)

we were waiting so long. He said, "The spirit has not arrived yet. I get a nudge from the spirit when he is here." At that moment, I was pushed in my shoulder, lifted into the air, and lowered back into the chair. I turned and looked behind, but it was empty and no one was there. He gave a great big smile and said, "Time to start."

One time while working, an enormously bulky man came for healing. The man's belly entered the room and led the way for the rest the body. The man said that he was unable to lose weight. He had tried dozens of diets, but he could never lose the bulk around his stomach. I stood by as Brother Roger opened him and began to extract thick masses of fat. The room smelled just like a butcher shop. This fat had lodged in the man's intestinal system, so it was understandable that no amount of dieting would have shifted it. During the operation, he placed the masses of fat into a plastic bucket, and after the man had left, by the way looking totally different, I lifted the bucket, and I estimated it weighed about eight to ten pounds. Astonishing!

Some of the conclusions I have drawn from observation and participation in Brother Roger's work have had a profound effect on my worldview. My first realization was that many of the debilitating diseases and the general decline in physical health that we associate with old age are not inevitable. They are the cumulative effects of decades of eating the wrong food, typically too much animal fat and red meat, with not enough fiber. Also, unresolved emotional issues that "eat away" at us eventually affect our physical body and make it difficult for people to emotionally compensate for physical pains and discomfort.

Working with Roger, I started to understand that tumors are not just lifeless masses of tissue. They possess a primal survival instinct, a natural drive of some kind. They are parasites and unable to exist outside the host. Tumors form in locations in the human organism where they are the most difficult to detect. From there they increasingly absorb nutrients from the body. Once they are sufficiently developed, they start to spread through the body and become detectable. These intelligent organisms, primed for "survival," are aware when they are disturbed or detected through an intrusive method such as a biopsy, and they respond to this by accelerating their growth and expansion by invading other parts of the body. This migration throughout the body is called metastasis. Many anecdotal narratives describe how tumors proliferate shortly after a biopsy. A tumor perfectly fits the shamanic definition regarding the cause of illness: an external intrusive form of energy enters the human energy template and creates a dissonance in the bioenergy pattern, which manifests in physical matter as an illness.

Perhaps we could regard tumors in a different way than the viewpoint of conventional medicine. We might adopt a perspective that they are not inanimate forms, but are animate with distinct energy fields, and at that level they can be extracted or neutralized.

How do you rationally explain bare-hand surgery and the direct intervention of spirits? The nature of reality is a mystery. Quantum physicists are at a loss to explain phenomena that have been verified experimentally, such as *quantum entanglement*. Quantum entanglement describes the changed state of a particle that is *instantaneously* transmitted to a paired particle, which could be billions of light years distant. Einstein had huge trouble in accepting this and famously called it "spooky action at a distance."

This is a counterintuitive reality. Objective reality becomes in essence a flawed concept, and consciousness is an instrument in the creation of reality. Keeping this notion in mind, if we look at the basic purpose of a ritual, ceremony, or prayer, it is really to effect a change or influence the unfolding of reality. The desired change is usually to improve the circumstances for a person or group, typically healing or drawing in fortunate influences. When we pray, are we indeed invoking the power of a disincarnate supernatural force? Or are we applying the power of our consciousness to influence the transient probability waves that generate reality in time and space? From this perspective, the actions of healers and shamans are totally rational.

However, this doesn't mean that shamanism and psychic surgery can be explained in terms of modern physics. Psychic surgeons and shamans can effect change in local reality (e.g., their clients) through what is called "spiritual" power operating at the quantum level.

The process of psychic surgery is explained by a former professor of physics and chemistry at the University of Dortmund, Dr. Alfred Stelter. He defines the process of painless, bare-handed operation thus:

> The healers form strong etheric force or energy in their hands through intense concentration. This energy penetrates matter at the cellular or even sub-atomic levels where matter and energy are interchangeable. After the accumulation of etheric forces, the magnetic cohesive energy (force that holds the cells of the bodies together) is separated through unpolarization. And then after the operation, the cells go back to their former appearance.[2]

Our inability to rationally understand, define, or explain bare-hand surgery is not relevant. As the sages and wise ones say, "The proof of the pudding is in the eating," and in the years that I have been working and researching in the Philippines, I have come to understand it in that manner. The psychic surgeons and shamans certainly do not see their work in measurable scientific terms. Striving for rational explanations prevents us from entering this mysterious world.

# 12

# THE SHAMAN AS ARTIST AND CREATOR

*Now, I'm sure that we couldn't carry out a discussion of this sort without observing that the prototypic figure for the artist, as well as for the scientist, is the shaman. The shaman is the figure at the beginning of human history that unites the doctor, the scientist, and the artist into a single notion of care-giving and creativity. And I think that, you know, to whatever degree art, over the past several centuries, has wandered in the desert, it is because this shamanic function has been either suppressed or forgotten.*

TERENCE MCKENNA, FROM A TALK IN PORT
HEUNEME, CALIFORNIA, SPONSORED BY THE
CARNEGIE MUSEUM OF ART, EARLY 1990S

In the 1980s, PBS broadcast the landmark series *The Power of Myth* with Bill Moyers interviewing Joseph Campbell. Many of the conversations dealt with the journey of the shaman from a mythic perspective. In one such discussion, Moyers asks, "Who interprets the divinity inherent in nature for us today? Who are our shamans? Who interprets unseen things for us?"

Campbell responds, "It is the function of the artist to do this. The artist is the one who communicates myth for today. Artists provide the contemporary metaphors that allow us to realize the transcendent, infinite, and abundant nature of being as it is."[1]

Campbell and Moyers are putting forth the concept that the *act of creation* is the precise locus where the shaman and artist meet. The act of creation makes an intangible idea or vision manifest in the world. In this act we have a meeting of two realms of consciousness, the transcendent and the physical.

This act of creation can be a vision or an idea that transforms the world. In this act of creation, the artificial boundaries between art, science, and the mystical experience are erased. What can follow is a totally new way of seeing the world. The pioneering mathematician Benoit Mandelbrot introduced to humanity a novel way to perceive reality through his discovery of fractal geometry. Fractals are repeating patterns of expanding symmetry that flow through the cosmos from the infinitesimal to the astronomical scale.

From a mathematical perspective, fractals are feedback loops of matter, or energy, and they underlie structural patterns of nature and in fact consciousness. This is the great revelation of science, shamans, and art.

Normally, "vision" is an optical metaphor; the phenomenon of light reflected from an object is *albedo* light. This light is directly perceivable energy reflected from a surface or emitted by an object such as a light bulb onto the retina. In the act of creation, moving from the unmanifest into the manifest, we enter the mysterious domain of *nonalbedo* light. This light is seen in the mind's eye during dreams, visions, meditation, or when using the imagination.

Arguably, one of the most important scientific discoveries of the twentieth century was Einstein's special theory of relativity. For a decade Einstein struggled to reconcile the fundamental inconsistencies between the two pillars of physics, namely Newton's law of gravitation and James Maxwell's theory of electromagnetism. The basic problem that Einstein was attempting to resolve was that both could not be right. One day he gave up and returned exhausted to his home in the center of Bern; he had decided to give up the entire inquiry. Then in the evening, he allowed his mind to enter into a daydream. He called these mind wanderings *thought experiments*. In this daydream, or visionary state of consciousness, he saw a tram accelerating away from the famous city clock tower at the speed of light. He saw himself inside the tram, and when he looked back at the clock, it had stopped. He realized that to someone outside the tram, the clock would appear to be functioning normally. This was an epiphany, a revelation. In a flash he realized that the notion of space and time as separate things was wrong; they are in fact one thing: *spacetime*. This vision changed our world. It heralded a new era of physics, a new understanding of consciousness, and a new way of perceiving the universe.

The creative visionary experience unifies the separate domains of the arts and science. The visionary experience opens the doors to the great mystery. In many respects, it defines the act of creation, an act that inspires us to look beyond the veil of cultural and linguistic limitations. This act alone has the potential to transform and evolve human consciousness. Both science and art have shown us that the illusion of duality is just that, an illusion, that is, the creator is not separate from creation. As Ra Bonewitz states in his book *The Cosmic Crystal Spiral,* "science is the branch of mysticism that deals with the measurable."[2]

The shaman is not just an artist in the traditional sense of musician, dramatist, painter, ritualist, singer, or ceremonialist (though he or she may be all of those things). The shaman is in touch with the creative energies of the entire universe. The shaman's life is a work of art, touching the infinite and transforming its powers into a new way of being for all of humanity. This is expressed not just in "art forms" but in the living art of the shaman's life. Both the shaman and the artist, through inspiration and the visionary state of consciousness, are able to access and communicate concepts from beyond everyday perceptions and to manifest their personal creative vision in the world, thus enriching their lives and the lives of others.

The notion that we have to learn creativity is a disempowering misunderstanding. Creativity is part of our intrinsic nature, and through us the primordial energy of the universal consciousness finds expression and becomes manifest. However, for many of us, due to the vicissitudes of life, the education system, and the overall institutional, homogenizing Western culture, an ersatz boundary has been constructed. A belief has arisen that we as individuals are not creative and that creativity is restricted to an exclusive creative elite of designers, architects, and artists.

In our society we are subject to the insidious influence of corporations, politicians, and their exploitative media lackeys, who have the objective to keep us in a *low-vibrational* material state of consciousness so that we remain consumers and, of course, debtors. Their arsenal is filled with mind-numbing spirit "sedatives," such as television programs, shiny new electronic gadgets, and, last but not least, sugar.*

The high levels of refined sugar added to processed foods and soft drinks are pernicious. The detrimental effects of diabetes and obesity caused by refined sugar are well known. From a neurological outlook, refined sugar is a drug and operates much the same way as addictive drugs such as cocaine and heroin, by releasing high levels of dopamine and other opioids into the brain. Dopamine is a neurotransmitter, and one of its primary characteristics is the activation of the "pleasure-reward" response: you have that good, pleasurable feeling which encourages you to repeat the sugar intake, thus starting an addiction cycle. We are conditioned to receive a reward of something sweet such as candy when we are children because we have behaved in an appropriate way or accomplished a task that has pleased an adult. Looking at this from a creative consciousness perspective, refined sugar makes us "sweet,"

---

*A good resource for more information on the addictive characteristics of sugar is the following book: Dr. Robert Lustig, *Fat Chance: The Hidden Truth about Sugar, Obesity and Disease* (London: Fourth Estate, 2014).

placid, and controllable. It is in the interests of the dominator system to keep its citizens in this material, obedient consciousness. By freeing yourself of refined sugar in foods and drinks you are also freeing your unique creativity, in other words, your *soul* freedom.

We live in a totally new paradigm that was unimaginable to most of our forebears at the end of the nineteenth century. With relativity and quantum mechanics, physics entered into a new and vast conceptual universe. The world has made so many discoveries in the last one hundred years that it is impossible to even think of listing them in this book, so I will talk about just one discovery that has influenced all our lives. It is at the same time miraculous yet so ubiquitous we hardly think about it. I am referring to music.

When I came across Internet radio, I was amazed at the enormous number and variety of stations—dedicated to a single band, singers, particular genres, and so on. Then I realized that until Emile Berliner invented the gramophone in 1887, the possibility of hearing recorded music simply did not exist. People had to go where the music was being played, so this meant that they may have heard a piece of music that they loved just a few times, *if that,* in their life.

Interestingly, one of the defining characteristics of a tyrannical dictatorship is the censorship and control of music. In Romania I worked with a client who was imprisoned and *reeducated* for the heinous crime of listening to the Rolling Stones. I was shocked to hear this, yet it was heartwarming to hear stories of how people worked around this insanity by illicitly recording music on tape and sharing it. Music is liberation; it moves the body and soul.

In my view, music is the medicine to heal the suppression of the creative soul. Maybe one day music could take the place of religion. Music is an expression of the human spirit, something that we all share and that unites us; it is uplifting and connects us to the source of creation itself. Visionaries such as Nikola Tesla, Rudolf Steiner, and Pablo Amaringo clearly saw this. Pablo said: "Music is very special; it is the expression of joy; it can imbue you with the flame of passion. All that has been brought into existence, the stars and the cosmos, is created by music and sound. Since it deeply influences our thinking and emotions, we should listen to music that inspires our highest humanity."[3] The understanding of a universal language of light, sound, color, and vibration and their relationship to form and matter is pure visionary thinking. Visionary arts, science, shamanism, meditation, and other spiritual practices are conduits between the material world and the transpersonal field of consciousness that provide a means for us to connect to the creative source of all things.

One of the greatest actions we can take in releasing our innate creativity is to see the world like we did as children. All of us as children are fully immersed, even enthralled, in the creative macrocosm. Watching my daughter Katie see a rose for the first time is forever etched in my memory. She was truly captivated by its form, color, and scent. In a state of bliss, she gently moved her hands around the flower, and without actually touching, she embraced the blossom. It was a sublime experience to witness this wondrous moment. This is where we adults can learn from children; in our hurried, stressful lives, we have become immune to the wonder and celestial majesty of the natural world. We have forgotten the incontrovertible fact that at one time in our lives we too saw, smelled, tasted, and heard something for the very first time. On the road to being a respectable citizen many have lost this profound state of wonder.

At my workshop "The Shaman as Artist and Creator," I present a six-stage series of creative enrichment exercises. These practices are structured to bring the mind-body system into alignment with the primordial creative source, to dissolve the inner blocks to creativity, and to act as a catalyst for the individual's creative alchemy. Although it is convenient to list them sequentially, these practices actually form an intrinsic geometric structure.

Participants have written to tell me how opening their creativity has helped them in their lives. Alexandra from Bucharest describes the transformative power of opening to her inner creativity:

*I've been working for nine years in creative industries, and at the time I participated in this workshop, I didn't understand what creativity really meant and never knew where to look for my own. Even though my job supposedly means being creative every day, I never knew what it meant to put creative energy in the things you do until I was part of this workshop. I painted for the first time, I sang, I read in stones, I traveled with the help of my imagination to places I had never visited before, and I continue to do all these things whenever I connect to my creative energy. Maybe the most important thing I learned is that this energy resides in each of us; it comes from within every time we set our intention, and it helps us shape our lives and be true to ourselves. Today I work on building my own business; my path and my passions are much clearer to me; I dance expressing my emotions; and I create my life as I want to live it.*

Danina, also from Bucharest, describes her experience:

*I was never an artistic creature. I graduated in construction engineering, and I grew up knowing that I am not talented in any way. Now I draw mandalas, I paint stones, I dance, I write, I sing. Each empowerment that I received helped me bring back a huge quantity of vital energy, energy that was blocked in beliefs like "I am not creative" and "I have nothing to say.*

## OVERVIEW OF THE SIX CREATIVE ENRICHMENT PRACTICES

1. Align the mind-body system with the universal creative source.
2. Dissolve the inner obstacles to creativity.
3. Encounter the archetype of primordial creativity.
4. See the world like a child again.
5. Discover the luminous symbol of your creative power.
6. Manifest your creative energy.

From a geometric perspective the practices are not linear but have an interconnected relationship (see color plate 12). Following this primordial creative template, undertake one practice each day for six days. All of the creative enrichment practices are presented in the first person.

It is a useful discipline to make notes or draw sketches of your experiences to assist you in grounding your visions.

## FIRST CREATIVE ENRICHMENT PRACTICE

### ✳ Align the Mind-Body System with the Universal Creative Source

To begin with, find a place where you feel comfortable and will not be disturbed for about an hour. When you are ready, either lie down or sit in a comfortable chair and darken the room, or at least cover your eyes. (It is easier to carry out this type of visionary work in subdued light.) Remove or release any tight or restrictive clothing, and allow your breathing to move to a gentle rhythm. As you breathe allow yourself to feel rooted or perhaps feel a kind of magnetic pull to the ground. This empowering meditation was gifted to me by John-Richard Turner, founder of the body of work called the Prebirth Analysis Matrix, with whom I studied in the 1980s.

The purpose of this practice is to open the mind and body to the spiritual essence of creation and to prepare for the subsequent practices. This is the primary alignment to open your soul radiance to the full spectrum of universal interconnectedness and the divine.

Say the following to yourself as you relax:

I am aware of radiance in my toes.

I am aware of radiance in my feet.

I am aware of radiance in my ankles.

I am aware of radiance in my shins and my calves.

I am aware of radiance in my knees.

I am aware of radiance in my thighs and my hips.

I am aware of radiance in my abdomen.

I am aware of radiance in my solar plexus.

I am aware of radiance in my chest.

I am aware of radiance in my spine.

I am aware of radiance at the base of my spine.

And very gently . . .

I bring my awareness of this radiance up my spine to the top of my head. Using my creative imagination I make a little opening at the top of my head. I let my awareness move through this opening, and I let it go instantly to the center of creation, wherever that is, simply by willing it to be there. The words are "I will to be at the center of creation NOW!" (For many people, the center of creation is sensed about six inches above the head.)

And as I arrive at this point of consciousness, I see that all of creation is filled with this radiance . . . this light . . . this illumination . . . pulsing . . . shimmering . . . vibrating. I let myself be enveloped in this radiance . . . embraced in this radiance . . . I merge with this radiance. . . .

I become one with this radiance. As I do, I realize that this radiance is the creative force of all light, and this force has many names. But one name I can give it is unconditional love, the unconditional love of creation for all of itself. And because I share in this creation, am a part of this creation, I know that I share in this unconditional love.

And now, I draw this light down through the top of my head into my brain center. I let the consciousness of all the cells in my brain receive this radiance as a gift from myself for functioning perfectly.

I let this radiance flow into my forehead area, and I let the consciousness of all the cells in my forehead receive this radiance as a gift from myself for giving me perfect inner vision, perfect insight. (This is often experienced as a very physical feeling, a tingling or pulsing in the center of the forehead, as inner vision gently opens and strengthens.)

And now I let this light flow through my eyes . . . my optic nerves . . . my nose . . . my sinuses . . . my ears . . . my mouth . . . and my throat. I let the consciousness of all the sense organs in my head receive this radiance as a gift from myself for functioning perfectly.

I let this radiance flow down my arms into my open hands, and after a moment, I turn my palms upward. I let the consciousness of all the cells in my hands receive this radiance as a gift from myself for giving me a perfect touch ... a perfect creativity ... a perfect strength. (This is often experienced as a very physical feeling.)

I realize that I am holding a radiant ball of healing crystal light in the palms and the fingertips of my hands. As I feel this healing light in my palms ... I know that I have brought this healing light to the consciousness of every cell in my body. It is simply that in my hands I can feel it very clearly.

And now I offer this healing light to all those who have requested help or healing from me ... that each may use it in whatever way is most appropriate for that person's evolution. I see or think of each person.

I offer this healing light to all those whose names do not come to me at this moment ... that those people too may share in its benefits. I offer this healing light to all those who have died ... that each may use it in whatever way is most appropriate for that person's evolution. I see or think of each person.

I offer this healing light to all those whom I have loved, love now, or ever will love. I see or think of each person. I offer this healing light to all those whom I have loved, love now, or ever will love whose names do not come to me at this moment ... that those people too may share in its benefits.

Now I offer this healing light into my own heart center. I let the consciousness of all the cells in my heart receive this light as a gift from myself for giving me perfect, unconditional self-love ... perfect, unconditional love of myself. And I feel joy in my heart as it realizes that I have actually merged back with the source of my own being ... that I am no longer alone but connected with this source.

I thank my heart for pumping the life blood through my body every moment of this life; I am no longer alone but connected with that source. With each beat of my heart, not only is it pumping the blood but it is also spreading this radiance to my lungs ... to my breasts ... to my solar plexus ... and to my abdomen.

I let the consciousness of all the cells ... the organs ... the glands ... the muscles ... and the bones receive this radiance as a gift from myself for functioning perfectly. I let this healing radiance flow down over my head … my face … my shoulders … and my back, and I realize that I am sitting in a cascade of radiant healing light, which is flowing in, through, and around my whole self.

I know that I can renew this energy whenever I want. I let it flow over my hips and thighs … my knees … my shins … my calves … my ankles … my feet … and my toes. And because I have been very conscious and very wide awake … when I want, I can gently open my eyes.

## SECOND CREATIVE ENRICHMENT PRACTICE

## ✳ Dissolve the Inner Obstacles to Creativity

To begin with, find a place where you feel comfortable and will not be disturbed for about an hour. When you are ready, either lie down or sit in a comfortable chair and darken the room, or at least cover your eyes. (It is easier to carry out this type of visionary work in subdued light.) Remove or release any tight or restrictive clothing, and allow your breathing to move to a gentle rhythm. As you breathe allow yourself to feel rooted or perhaps feel a kind of magnetic pull to the ground.

The purpose of this practice is to release the nonconscious, disempowering energies that over time have become entangled with your luminous soul essence. These are the judgments that others have made and, of course, your own self-judgments. These judgments are a diminishing negative energy that has calcified and becomes intractable over time. These are the so-called blocks to our soul essence. Typical judgments are: "Who do you think you are?" "I can't do this," and "I'm useless." These messages infiltrate our mind-body system and sentence us to live our life within these limitations. It is part of the "original sin" paradigm, which holds that even as newborns, we are sinners, not good enough. This paradigm—a bedrock of Western culture—has established an insidious pattern of disempowerment and has undermined self-esteem, separating us from our inner creative power. We have the ability to free ourselves from this.

Say the following to yourself as you relax:

I start to gently breath, inhaling deep into the base of my stomach, and then after a second I gently exhale. I repeat this inhalation and exhalation six times. While I am breathing in this soft way, I simply allow the inner feelings to emerge, without any thought, without any judgment, without the inner disempowering messages from my life. . . . The unconscious obstacles that impede my primal creativity stir within me and arise.

I gently allow this energy to rise, and as I feel it move I expel it by blowing it out through my mouth like dark smoke. I blow this smoky substance into the space in front of me like a cloud, where it curls, swirls, and then dissipates and dissolves. I realize that this disempowering energy never had any substance in my life . . . and as I continue to breathe it out, I know in my heart that it had substance only because I allowed it to.

With each breath, I release this energy, and I know that I am now experiencing true freedom. Now I breathe in through my nostrils a rainbow-colored light. This rainbow light is the quintessence of grace, wisdom, and an empowering, revitalizing energy that permeates my entire body, from the soles of my feet to the crown of my head, becoming centered in my heart.

Now from my heart I project this rainbow healing and purifying light into the space in front of me, where it becomes in my mind's eye a luminous and vibrating sphere of radiance.

I now open my mouth wide, and I make the sound "aah," and with this vibration I manifest this radiant sphere into the world. I know it is the primordial, universal energy of creativity, and I know that I too am part of this divine imagination. I know that my separation from the source of universal creative power was only an illusion.

Again I make the sound "aah," and this light moves into my third eye in my forehead, infusing and empowering my creative spirit. I know that the primordial divine creative energy is being expressed through me and that I am no longer disconnected from this source. I pledge to manifest this energy in ways that heal and bring benefit to myself and to others.

## ✳ Encounter the Embodiment of Primordial Creativity

To begin with, find a place where you feel comfortable and will not be disturbed for about an hour. When you are ready, either lie down or sit in a comfortable chair and darken the room, or at least cover your eyes. (It is easier to carry out this type of visionary work in subdued light.) Remove or release any tight or restrictive clothing, and allow your breathing to move to a gentle rhythm. As you breathe allow yourself to feel rooted or perhaps feel a kind of magnetic pull to the ground. Focus now on the first principle of intention. Concentrate on your intention as you align your energy with thought and outcome.

The purpose of this practice is to journey to the upper world to encounter the embodiment of primordial creativity. This practice draws upon the quintessential archetype of the being who has gone beyond conventional human bounds and has attained deep wisdom. This is the epitome of the spiritual master. This encounter with the master can actuate your creativity and empower your vision.

Say the following to yourself as you relax:

In my creative imagination I allow myself to go to a location I know of that reminds me of Earth. In this location I will find a place where I can go up, or climb. It could be a tree, a mountain, a hill, or a pyramid, and I will recognize this place where I can ascend. I possess a strong sense of being present in this location, and I gently relax and feel increasingly comfortable.

I now see the place where I can go up, and I start to make my ascent. During this ascent I am aware of passing through an ethereal layer, with the texture of tissue paper or clouds. I know that this is the separator between realms, and as I move through it I arrive in the upper world. Here I am totally present; I am totally aware; I am totally conscious; and I gradually become increasingly aware of the colors, the sounds, the scents, and the movement of the air around me.

I now begin to explore, and with all of my sensory faculties functioning in a heightened state, I soon know where I need to go to encounter the embodiment of primordial creativity. (This embodiment can be in any form, shape, or size. It could be a water fountain, a crystal, a cloud of spiral particles, or a field of colored energy, or it could be personified in the form of a master or celestial being.) I will recognize the form and substance of the creative energy.

At this time there is nothing to do but to be present with the source of primordial creative energy and allow its sublime essence to infuse and merge with my being. During this I may receive inspirational imagery, hear elevating words, or just feel embraced by the source of divine creativity.

When I feel ready and my being is filled with this transcendent creative energy, I will speak words of gratitude and appreciation. Now it is time to return to the manifest world. The creative energy from the primordial source is now within me.

## ✛ Coming Back

This is all important and needs to be integrated into your intention, either spoken or unspoken. This work has no point unless you come back into the physical world so you can build your bridge between the manifest and the unmanifest realities.

Return to everyday reality either by setting a prearranged time with a drumming friend or using the call-back drumming rhythm on a shamanic journeying track. Coming back requires volition and discipline because you may be in a place from which you do not want to return. When you hear the call-back signal, stop what you are doing, say your farewells, turn around, and return the same way that you came. Make your descent, and when you have arrived in the place that you started from, the place in your imagination that reminded you of Earth, become aware of that place, feel your feet on the ground, and sense the ground pushing up against the soles of your feet. Be back in the physical world.

### FOURTH CREATIVE ENRICHMENT PRACTICE

## ✳ See the World like a Child Again

In this practice, we reach back through our lives to a time when everything was new, magical, and filled with wonder. Time in this practice is not linear, and rather than just recapturing a memory, we reincorporate the extraordinary and miraculous experience of being *our* magical child. We go back to a time when the surrounding world was unstructured by linguistic form and we experienced the world through sensory systems without the mediating influence of language.

To begin with, find a place where you feel comfortable and will not be disturbed for about an hour. When you are ready, either lie down or sit in a comfortable chair and darken the room, or at least cover your eyes. (It is easier to carry out this type of visionary work in subdued light.) Remove or release any tight or restrictive clothing, and allow your breathing to move to a gentle rhythm. As you breathe allow yourself to feel rooted or perhaps feel a kind of magnetic pull to the ground.

Focus now on the first principle of intention. Concentrate on your intention as you align your energy with thought and outcome. For the purposes of this practice, the intention is to journey to the lower world to experience the wonder of life through your magical inner child.

Say the following to yourself as you relax:

In my creative imagination I allow myself to go to a location that I know of that reminds me of Earth. In this location I will find a place where I can go down, or descend. It could be a cave entrance, a hole in the ground, an animal burrow, a body of water, or a well shaft, and I will recognize this entrance.

I possess a strong sense of being present in this location, and I gently relax and feel increasingly comfortable. I focus my intention to encounter my magical child as I move into the entrance and make my way down to the lower world, the place of nurturing and connection to the primordial mother, the Earth.

When I arrive in the lower world, I feel a sense of being present. My feet are firmly on the ground, and I sense the ground pushing up against the soles of my feet. I feel the wind around me; I can hear it blow through the trees. I hear the sound of rushing, flowing water. It could be a river, a stream, a waterfall, a fountain, a sea, or an ocean. As I stand there, I know that all my senses are functioning at an optimum level—my vision, my hearing, my sense of smell, and my sense of touch. I fully embrace my sensory experience as I am drawn to the presence of my magical child. I allow myself to become fully receptive to the miraculous, enchanting, endearing, lovable, engaging, and heavenly being that I am.

I realize that my magical child and I were never separate; that separation was only an illusion, a mirage. This sacred energy has always been a part of me. I allow the experience of being that child envelop me. My mind remembers, my body remembers, my soul memories return, and I recall and reexperience what it felt like the first time I saw a flower . . . the first time I smelled the perfume of a flower . . . the first time I heard music. . . the first time I saw clouds . . . the first time I was in the rain . . . the first time I smelled the grass after it had been raining . . . the first time I saw the color yellow . . . the first time I saw the color red . . . the first time I saw the color blue . . . the first time I saw a tree . . . the first time I laughed because I was happy . . . the first time I cried because I was sad. . . .

As I relive these experiences, I gently and lovingly allow all these feelings to reenter my conscious mind and body and be absorbed.

Now it is time to return to the manifest world and to bring back this sacred child that is now a part of me. When I return I pledge to bring a child-like beauty and innocence into my life for the benefit of myself and for the benefit of others.

I give my thanks and blessings to the magical child, and I go back along the path to where I started this journey, and because I have been fully conscious and wide awake, I gently open my eyes and return to the present. I realize that I am the same person, but I have changed. I have transformed into my whole self—the sublime combination of inner child and adult.

## FIFTH CREATIVE ENRICHMENT PRACTICE

## ✳ Discover the Luminous Symbol of Your Creative Power

This practice guides you to discover the symbol of your innate creative potential. It will have the effect of a magnetic attraction force that draws in your personal creative power from the transcendent and transpersonal realm.

Let's look for a moment at what a symbol actually is. Although there are a number of definitions, one unifying idea is that a symbol is not a sign. A sign is an indicator of something that is already known, such as traffic signs; signs that provide information, such as "Exit" signs; and increasingly signs that prohibit a specific activity, like "No Skateboarding." A symbol is something very different; it represents energy, a quality that stands in both the unmanifest and manifest realms of consciousness. It functions as a bridge between the two or a locus between the universal flow of creativity and human consciousness. Symbols are not static; they possess flow, motion. They are a luminous ordering of universal patterns that can enrich our hearts and minds. A symbol is a manifestation of the living cosmos that unites us with the primordial patterns of nature; it is a way to make the invisible energies of creation visible.

Each of us has a unique pattern that is woven throughout nature, which itself is a web of interconnected patterns. In this practice you will experience your unique pattern, a unique design interwoven in your soul. This is your personal symbol drawn down from the collective consciousness.

To begin with, find a place where you feel comfortable and will not be disturbed for about an hour. When you are ready, either lie down or sit in a comfortable chair and darken the room, or at least cover your eyes. (It is easier to carry out this type of visionary work in subdued light.) Remove or release any tight or restrictive clothing, and allow your breathing to move to a gentle rhythm. As you breathe allow yourself to feel rooted or perhaps feel a kind of magnetic pull to the ground.

Focus now on the first principle of intention. Concentrate on your intention as you align your energy with thought and outcome. For the purposes of this practice, the intention is to journey to the upper world to discover the luminous symbol of your creative power.

Say the following to yourself as you relax:

In my creative imagination I allow myself to go to a location that I know of that reminds me of Earth. In this location I will find a place where I can go up, or climb. It could be a tree, a mountain, a hill, or a pyramid, and I will recognize this place where I can ascend. I possess a strong sense of being present in this location, and I gently relax and feel increasingly comfortable.

I now see the place where I can go up, and I start to make my ascent. During this ascent I am aware of passing through an ethereal layer, with the texture of tissue paper or clouds. I know that this is the separator between realms, and as I move through this I arrive in the upper world. Here I am totally present, I am totally aware, I am totally conscious, and I gradually notice the colors, the sounds, the scents, and the movement of the air around me.

I now begin to explore, and because all of my sensory faculties are functioning in a heightened state, I soon know where I need to go to discover the luminous symbol of my creative power. This symbol can be in any form, any shape, or any size. It could be a stone, a tree, a flower, a crystal, or a word. Typically, it would be something tangible, a sacred object that I could hold, and I know that even if it is large, as I reach out to touch it, the sacred object will reduce in size and I will be able to hold it in my hands. My heart will recognize this luminous symbol as being totally perfect for me.

And now I hold this sacred object in my hands, and as I do this, I bring this luminous symbol to my heart, where it becomes absorbed into my being. I know now that I have entered into a true communion with the divine energy of spirit. I allow these waves of consciousness to move throughout my body, informing every cell in my body, and I sense as this energy flows to my forehead that my creative visionary faculty, my third eye, gently opens like a shining flower of many petals.

At this time there is nothing to do but to be present and allow the sublime essence of the symbol to infuse and merge with my being. During this I may receive inspirational imagery, hear elevating words, or just feel embraced by this divine creativity.

When I feel ready and my being is filled with this transcendent creative energy, I will speak words of gratitude and appreciation. It is time to return to the manifest world, knowing that this symbol, this locus of creative energy from the primordial source, is now within me.

When you return from this journey, it is a productive practice to paint your symbol on a stone, a physical reminder of the symbol of your personal creative power.

SIXTH CREATIVE ENRICHMENT PRACTICE

## ✳ Manifest Your Creative Energy

Grounding or manifesting your vision is a fundamental tenet of shamanism. Unless your vision is brought into the world, it has no power. This has important implications; for example, if you have a vision that offers you the potential to change the course of your life, and you do not act on or implement this vision, then it remains a vision with unrealized potential. The purpose of a vision is to realize it in your life, nothing more and nothing less. To manifest your vision, to give it birth into the world, is often the most challenging act. When you do this it is a true act of power. I recommend that you embark on this journey only when you feel the inner call to do so. In the words of Sun Bear, "Don't tell me your visions unless they grow corn."

In this journey you will receive insight, an understanding of how you can consummate your vision in your life. In the previous five creative enrichment practices, you opened up to your inner creative power and placed yourself in alignment with the universal creative consciousness. This practice will help you unleash the power of your vision into the manifest world. That is the ever-evolving cosmic dance of the shaman.

To begin with, find a place where you feel comfortable and will not be disturbed for about an hour. When you are ready, either lie down or sit in a comfortable chair and darken the room, or at least cover your eyes. (It is easier to carry out this type of visionary work in subdued light.) Remove or release any tight or restrictive clothing, and allow your breathing to move to a gentle rhythm. As you breathe allow yourself to feel rooted or perhaps feel a kind of magnetic pull to the ground.

Focus now on the first principle of intention. Concentrate on your intention as you align your energy with thought and outcome. For the purposes of this practice, the intention is to journey to the middle world to discover how to manifest your creative energy. From a shamanic perspective, the middle world is the energetic template of the physical world in which we live, and actions performed there have a direct influence on the physical world.

It is a useful discipline as with all the above practices to make notes or draw sketches of your experience to assist you in grounding your vision.

Say the following to yourself as you relax:

In my creative imagination I allow myself to go to a location that reminds me of Earth. I possess a strong sense of being present in this location, and I gently relax and feel increasingly comfortable. In this place I will find a gateway, which can be of any shape, form, or size. It could, for example, be a space between two rocks, a space between two trees, a traditional country gate, or a form of energy gateway. I will recognize this gateway, and when I move through it I will know I am in the middle world.

I now begin to explore, and because all of my sensory faculties are functioning in a heightened state, I soon know where I need to go to discover how to manifest my creative energy in the everyday world. As I remain present in this place, I realize that the sacred is all around us. It is in me and in nature, and I know that I am an expression of the primordial creative consciousness that is experiencing its creation through me. The language of this universal mind is perceived through geometric patterns of which my mind, my body, and my soul are a part. I understand that I do not have to do anything; I am already an element of the universal consciousness.

As I establish my presence in the middle world, I feel that my feet are connected to the ground and that the soles of my feet are like magnets grounding me to the Earth. I sense roots growing from the soles of my feet into the ground, drawing nurturing force into me. This force rises through my body and into my heart center. I raise my arms to the sky and draw down celestial energy, which permeates my entire body and meets the nurturing force of the Earth in my heart center. I am like a tree, standing strong and purposeful between the worlds, a focus of celestial and Earth energies. In this state of consciousness, I know that everything I do from this moment on will be an expression of my innate creative power and by extension the primordial creative power of the universal consciousness.

And now, because I am filled with this transcendent creative energy, I know it is time to return to the manifest world, the only realm where it can be expressed. I return to the gateway, and once I am through, I know that I am fully awake and alert. I open my eyes, and I am back in the physical world, ready to express my creative power in all the things I do.

## CONCLUSION

Allow your creativity to explode in a burst of illumination in the world. Follow the muse that fills your heart with passion. Listen to music that inspires your highest consciousness. Get out of the cities and into nature. You are not a sinner who must be penitent; you are a child, a part of the cosmos. Abstain from foods and drinks that suppress your creative force. Change your life; seek out new adventures. Practice kindness and compassion to all living beings, and live a gentle life. Let the beauty of your spirit be your endowment to the world. Become a conscious and transformative element in the conception of a new world.

"May the Force be with you."

# ✳

# NOTES

## FOREWORD

1. Thomas Moore, "The Salt of Soul, the Sulfur of Spirit," in *A Blue Fire: Selected Writings of James Hillman,* ed. Thomas Moore, 113 (New York: Harper Perennial, 1989).
2. Ibid., 112.

## INTRODUCTION

1. Howard G. Charing, Peter Cloudsley, and Pablo Amaringo, *The Ayahuasca Visions of Pablo Amaringo* (Rochester, Vt.: Inner Traditions, 2011), 84.

## CHAPTER 2.
## STARTING TO HEAL

1. Michael Harner speaking in 1991 at a workshop at the California Institute of Integral Studies in San Francisco, where I was working as his assistant.

## CHAPTER 3.
## MAPS OF REALITY

1. Quote from Steve Beyer's "Singing to the Plants" blog page: www.singingtotheplants.com/2007/12/eliades-shamanism (accessed 10/18/16).

2. Mircea Eliade, *Shamanism: Archaic Techniques of Ecstasy* (London: Penguin/Arkana, 1989), 5.
3. John G. Neihardt, *Black Elk Speaks,* repr. ed. (Lincoln: Bison Books/ University of Nebraska Press, 1988), 85.
4. Richard Evans Schultes, Albert Hofmann, and Christian Rätsch, *Plants of the Gods,* rev. ed. (Rochester, Vt.: Healing Arts Press, 2001), 156.
5. Benny Shanon quoted in *The Guardian,* www.theguardian.com/world /2008/mar/05/religion.israelandthepalestinians (accessed 10/18/16).

## CHAPTER 5.
## SOUL RETRIEVAL

1. Tenzin Wangyal Rinpoche, "Shamanism in the Native Bon Tradition of Tibet," *Sacred Hoop Magazine* 7 (1994).

## CHAPTER 6.
## YOUR REALITY IS SACROSANCT

1. The Oxford Dictionary, s.v. "belief."
2. Dr. Bernard Lown quoted in Eric Peper, "Compassionate Presence: Covert Training Invites Subtle Energies Insights," *Subtle Energies Magazine* 26, no. 2 (2015): 22.
3. Gustave M. Gilbert, *Nuremberg Diary* (New York: Farrar, Straus and Company, 1947), 278–79.
4. President George W. Bush in an address to a joint session of Congress on September 20, 2001.

## CHAPTER 7.
## THE CONTINUUM OF LIFE

1. Sogyal Rinpoche, *In the Mirror of Death* (London: Rider, 1992), 11.
2. Spoken directly by Don Eduardo to Leo Rutherford in the 1980s, who later informed me.
3. Theodore Roszak, "Descartes' Angel, Reflections on the True Art of Thinking," in *The Betrayal of Tradition: Essays on the Spiritual Crisis of Modernity,* ed. Harry Oldmeadow (Bloomington, Ind.: World Wisdom, 2005), 301.
4. Albert Einstein, from a letter of condolence to the Besso family sent on the death of Einstein's friend Michele Angelo Besso in March 1955.

5. Quoted in the BBC documentary "The Hidden Life of the Cell," in the *Our Secret Universe* series, www.bbc.co.uk/programmes/b01nln7d (accessed 10/21/16).

6. Conversation between Carl Sagan and the Dalai Lama 1991. Conversation available on video at: www.youtube.com/watch?v=s6mqQDwVEaw (accessed 10/18/16).

## CHAPTER 8.
## ENERGY MEDICINE

1. C. G. Jung, "The Philosophical Tree," in *Collected Works of C. G. Jung*, vol. 13, *Alchemical Studies*, 335 (Princeton, N.J.: Princeton University Press, 2000).

2. Howard G. Charing, Peter Cloudsley, and Pablo Amaringo, *The Ayahuasca Visions of Pablo Amaringo* (Rochester, Vt.: Inner Traditions, 2011), 127.

## CHAPTER 9.
## THE COLORS OF INFINITY

1. Howard G. Charing, Peter Cloudsley, and Pablo Amaringo, *The Ayahuasca Visions of Pablo Amaringo* (Rochester, Vt.: Inner Traditions, 2011), 172.

2. Ibid., 39.

3. Howard G. Charing, "Communion with the Infinite: The Visual Music of the Shipibo Tribe of the Amazon," *Sacred Hoop Magazine* 47 (2004): 30–33.

4. From the webpage of the Dolphin Communication Project, Port St. Lucie, Florida, www.dolphincommunicationproject.org/index.php /the-latest-buzz/the-dolphin-pod/item/94427-so-high-it-hertz (accessed 10/18/16).

5. Ted Thornhill, "We All Crave It, but Can You Stand the Silence," April 3, 2012, www.dailymail.co.uk/sciencetech/article-2124581/The-worlds -quietest-place-chamber-Orfield-Laboratories.html (accessed 10/20/16).

## CHAPTER 10.
## AYAHUASCA, ENTHEOGENS, AND SACRAMENTAL PLANTS

1. Communicated during an interview with Artidoro conducted by Peter Cloudsley and Howard G. Charing in 2003. Available online at:

www.scribd.com/doc/46540888/Interview-With-Ayahuasca-Shaman -Artidoro (accessed 10/18/16).

2. Peter Cloudsley and Howard G. Charing in a conversation with Javier Arevalo, Peru, 2001.

3. Javier Arevalo quoted in Peter Cloudsley and Howard G. Charing, "Love, Magic, and the Vine of the Soul," *Sacred Hoop Magazine* 36 (2002): 14.

## CHAPTER 11.
## HEALING AND SORCERY IN THE
## PHILIPPINES AND PERU

1. *Philippine Daily Inquirer,* July 30, 2007, vol. 22, no. 232.

2. Alfred Stelter, *Psi Healing* (New York: Bantam Books, 1977).

## CHAPTER 12.
## THE SHAMAN AS ARTIST AND CREATOR

1. Joseph Campbell, *The Power of Myth,* episode entitled "Sacrifice and Bliss." Available online at: billmoyers.com/content/ep-4-joseph -campbell-and-the-power-of-myth-sacrifice-and-bliss-audio (accessed 10/20/16).

2. Ra Bonewitz, *The Cosmic Crystal Spiral* (Loughborough, UK: Thoth Publications, 1986).

3. Howard G. Charing, Peter Cloudsley, and Pablo Amaringo, *The Ayahuasca Visions of Pablo Amaringo* (Rochester, Vt.: Inner Traditions, 2011), 97.

# ✳

# GLOSSARY

**curandera/curandero:** A traditional South American native healer or shaman. The term comes from the Spanish word *curar,* which means "to heal." A curandero works in a holistic way and may incorporate various healing practices including the use of medicinal plants, sacred ceremony, and spiritual and energy healing.

**diet (la dieta):** A discipline required of Amazonian shamans, healers, and apprentices who wish to learn directly from the plant spirits. It implies much more than the mere dietary restrictions of avoiding salt, sugar, meat, and alcohol. It also means refraining from libidinous thoughts and sexual activity. It is an extensive period of complete isolation for weeks, or even months, and often the apprentice must fend for himself in the wilderness.

**encantos:** Magical stones used by shamans for healing. Encantos possess hidden powers that can be combined with ícaros to heal.

**ícaros:** The word ícaro comes from the Quechua word *icarai,* meaning "to blow." Ícaros are magical chants that are sung or whistled by shamans during ayahuasca ceremonies. There are several kinds of ícaros. At the beginning of a ceremony, their purpose is to provoke the mareación, or visionary trance state, and to render the mind more susceptible for visions to penetrate. The shaman on his plant diet learns the ícaros directly from the plant spirits. Ícaros have great power, and they influence the visionary experience of people drinking ayahuasca in a ceremony. Pablo Amaringo regarded the ícaro as the sound of the universe—the planets, stars, comets, and supernovas. Everything is created by music, by vibration, by sound. Ícaros are the music of creation.

**mapacho:** This is the common name for *Nicotiana rustica,* a locally grown tobacco that is one of the most important plants used by shamans in the Amazon. It is used for protection during ayahuasca ceremonies, for intensifying the mareación, and for giving soplos for healing. It is usually smoked in large cigarettes as puros (rolled in leaves similar to cigars) or in a pipe (cashimbo). It is matured for long periods and macerated in aguar-diente (alcohol). It can be "dieted" and taken internally or added to the ayahuasca brew to encourage purging. It can also be used for dressing wounds.

**mareación:** The visionary and trance effects of ayahuasca, which may vary greatly and depend on many factors. It may be necessary to purge and purify before the ecstatic and beautiful visions can be experienced.

**ofrenda:** An ofrenda, or offering ceremony, is the most important ceremony used by Andean Indians to relate with Mother Earth. The ofrenda is a symbol of reciprocity with nature and nature's purpose and is an expression of gratitude, not of debt or obligation.

**psychopomp:** Meaning "guide of souls" or "conductor of souls." One of the roles of the shaman is to be a midwife to the dying. In that role the shaman helps to usher the soul, or essence, of the dying person into the unity of the afterlife.

**Quechua:** The indigenous language of the Andean region of Peru. It was the language spoken by the Inca.

**soplada:** From the Spanish for "to blow," *soplo,* or *soplada,* usually refers to the practice of blowing mapacho (tobacco) smoke onto a person. The smoke is directed onto specific parts of the patient. The soplada is an important part of healing and is typically used for cleansing and as a conduit for the shaman's concentration and energy.

# ✳

# INDEX

Numbers in *italics* indicate illustrations.
Numbers in *italics* preceded by *pl.* indicate colored plate numbers.

# BOOKS OF RELATED INTEREST

**Plant Spirit Shamanism**
Traditional Techniques for Healing the Soul
*by Ross Heaven and Howard G. Charing*
*Foreword by Pablo Amaringo*

**The Ayahuasca Visions of Pablo Amaringo**
*by Howard G. Charing, Peter Cloudsley, and Pablo Amaringo*

**Plant Intelligence and the Imaginal Realm**
Beyond the Doors of Perception into the Dreaming of Earth
*by Stephen Harrod Buhner*

**The Secret Teachings of Plants**
The Intelligence of the Heart in the Direct Perception of Nature
*by Stephen Harrod Buhner*

**Advanced Autogenic Training and Primal Awareness**
Techniques for Wellness, Deeper Connection to Nature, and Higher
Consciousness
*by James Endredy*

**Speaking with Nature**
Awakening to the Deep Wisdom of the Earth
*by Sandra Ingerman and Llyn Roberts*

**Shapeshifting**
Techniques for Global and Personal Transformation
*by John Perkins*

**The Gift of Shamanism**
Visionary Power, Ayahuasca Dreams, and Journeys to Other Realms
*by Itzhak Beery*
*Foreword by John Perkins*

INNER TRADITIONS • BEAR & COMPANY
P.O. Box 388
Rochester, VT 05767
1-800-246-8648
www.InnerTraditions.com

Or contact your local bookseller